TUSCANY AT THE TABLE

*Cooking Guide
for Gourmet Tourists*

TEMPO LIBERO

by sillabe

We would like to thank, for their precious contributions and friendly advice:
Salvatore Ammendola, Mamma Rosella and Papà Tobia, Marco Adami and Mamma Giovanna, Giulia Bastianelli and Nonna Emiliana, Biagio and Lorenza from the "La Bottega dei Gaudenti", Alessio Cecchi and Mamma Marisa, Paola Crema, Giovanna Gallo, Massimiliano Gambacciani, Clara Mancini, Rosanna Pecchioli, Melissa Sicurani and Nonna Dina, Francesca and Maria Pia Taviani with Mamma Milvia

Abbreviations and symbols
in. = inch(es)
hr. = hour(s)
min. = minute(s)
lb. = pound(s)
qt. = quart(s)
🍷 = recommended wine

Notes
The indication 'olive oil' always means the finest extra-virgin olive oil. The vanilla flavoring used in Italy comes in the form of a powder, for which you can substitute either vanilla extract or a stick of vanilla, also in the case of vanilla-flavored sugar and baking powder.

Opposite page:
ABRAHAM MIGNON, *Fruit and Objects on a Cabinet*, Florence, Galleria degli Uffizi (detail)

© 2008 **s i l l a b e** s.r.l.
Livorno
www.sillabe.it
info@sillabe.it

Managing editor: *Maddalena Paola Winspeare*
Texts: *Ethel Santacroce*
Translation: *Catherine Frost*
Graphic Design: *Fabrizio Bagatti*
Editing: *Giulia Bastianelli*
Coordination: *Laura Belforte*
Cartography: *Studio Caba & Chesi*
Photo Credits: *Archivio Sillabe: Foto G. Andreini, N. Bianchini, B. Bruchi, C. Cascioli, S. Casini, A. Chiarini, C. Corrivetti, M. Gambacciani, Foto Lensini, A. Nowacki, C. Olivieri, T. Rusmi, N. Salvadorini, M. Sicurani; Archivio Felix Productions.*
The publisher is at the disposal of the copyright holders of images from unidentified sources.

ISBN 978-88-8347-461-3

TUSCANY AT THE TABLE

Geographically speaking, the region of Tuscany encompasses a large area that, starting from the Apennine mountains, stretches across the central hills and valleys, to arrive at the Tyrrhenian coast; and so it is only logical to think that this territorial diversity will be matched by gastronomical variety. Historically too, its cuisine is deeply rooted in the long-past Etruscan culture (whose strong influence is still felt today in the territories of Arezzo, Siena and the Maremma bordering on Lazio) and in that of the ancient Romans. Often defined as 'a cuisine with no frills', Tuscan cooking is simple, balanced and genuine, the distinctive characteristics of a peasant civilization that can still be felt in its various dishes, enriched with sobriety and never with excess. A tradition linked to the seasons, to hard work in the fields, to the raising of cattle, sheep and goats and to fishing along the coastline, when Tuscan housewives had at their disposal the products of the earth, the sea and the forest, as well as great skill in transforming leftovers into tasty, original dishes; such as **ribollita,** made of stale bread that had to last for several days; and the **acquacotta** of Maremma, consisting basically of water and eggs; and even the **brodo di sassi** (stone soup) of Livorno, made with water and stones from the sea.
The region can boast one of the world's most wholesome and genuine basic ingredients: extra-virgin olive oil, slightly fruity with a pungent taste, which adapts perfectly to any dish. It varies from one zone to another, and many of these have won important recognition such as the DOP (certificate of protected denomination of origin). Another important element is bread, traditionally salt-free,

which becomes sweet for festivities, transformed into **pasimata**, **buccellato** and **pan di ramerino**. And not to be forgotten is **schiacciata**, a flat loaf, salty and gleaming with olive oil, excellent with the typical Tuscan charcuterie or even alone as a snack; while in the mountainous areas (Lunigiana, Casentino, and Garfagnana) are found various kinds of bread enriched which chestnut flour or potatoes. And the meat and fish used to make one-dish meals, or as either first or second courses, such as a good portion of **peposo** from Florence, **garmugia** from Lucca, **cacciucco** from Livorno or **scottiglia** from Casentino (Arezzo) as well as seasonal products such as vegetables and legumes.

In spite of its sobriety, Tuscan cooking is also refined, offering an array of sophisticated, unusual combinations boasting ancient origins (for example, **cibreo**, **papero al melarancio** and **lepre in dolceforte**). And then there is the famous **bistecca di manzo**, an amazingly thick T-bone grilled very rare. Then come soups, made mostly of vegetables and legumes. Specifically, the Florentines are called "mangiafagioli" (bean-eaters) for their love of these legumes, widely consumed in the many different species grown in the region. There are in fact over thirty different types, the most famous of which are the "Cannellino", the "Zolfino" and the black-eyed pea, excellent when cooked **al fiasco** or **all'uccelletto**.

Sweets vary depending on the season, offering a wide range of choices, both for true gourmands who prefer the richer, more elaborate recipes – **zuccotto**, **torta della nonna** and **torta al semolino** first among them – and more basic, such as **biscotti** and **cantuccini** from Prato e and **castagnaccio** for those who want simplicity; in any case, all of them are absolutely worth sampling.

A brief introduction to the origins of this cuisine will be useful at this point, for a better appreciation of its flavors.

The Etruscans and the Romans

As noted above, the Etruscans are the ancestors of the Tuscans of today; but no written evidence of their recipes exists. Only from the findings unearthed and safeguarded in museums can be deduced the customs that give us an idea of how important dining was for them (famous in fact are the archeological findings – vases, cinerary urns, amphorae and tableware – bearing scenes of kitchens, banquets with men and women stretched out on divans, tables set for a banquet, scenes of hunting and fishing) and how often their banquets were accompanied by dancing and music. Their enormous talent for trade and establishing contacts with distant peoples such as the Greeks favored culinary exchange as well and, like most of the ancient populations, the Etruscans too lived on hunting, fishing, stockbreeding and agriculture.

From all of this derives the wealth of ingredients such as olive oil, eggs, cereals, vegetables both wild and cultivated, milk to make cheese, fish, wine, honey and so on, which were at the basis of a refined, delicious cuisine. The Etruscans were also the first to introduce many of the foods that have come down to us, for instance such cereals as "farro" (**minestra di farro** was already in use) and **orzo.** And they have even been thought to have created the first pasta dish: **pici.** Highly important was the raising of pigs – no part of which was thrown away, then as now. And most important, they are thought to have been the first to preserve pork by salting it, thus creating a primitive version of cured prosciutto. And it seems that they also invented **porchetta.** Moreover, they also raised the famous breed of cattle called **Chianina**, known today for its equally famous steaks. We know that they ate meat not only roasted but also boiled and frequently cooked in olive oil, or in elaborate recipes enriched with such ingredients as honey, herbs, wine, a kind of primitive yogurt made of fermented milk, and *liquamen*, a sauce made of little fish left to ferment in the sun for months and used as dressing for practically everything, equally popular with the Romans. They accompanied their foods with various types of bread, made mostly of barley and "farro" and they used polenta (still today in Garfagnana it is customary to cook it with meat) and chestnut flour, as well as legumes such as chickpeas, lentils and broad beans.

The Romans, instead, had a less refined cuisine and only after having conquered the Etruscan territory did they learn from this people the art of cooking, so that they refined and enriched their recipes with elaborate preparations and techniques, and many texts on the subject of cooking have come down to us.

We have anecdotes of splendid Lucullian banquets with lavishly scenographic dishes and combinations of foods deemed extravagant today. They also used the spices (pepper, cinnamon and cumin) that arrived from the Orient to mask the strong smells of meat dishes, which deteriorated rapidly. For them, as for the Etruscans, dining together was a very important moment for doing business and forming alliances, as well as for the pure taste of the food. This was true especially of the wealthier classes. But even the poorer ones had available a considerable variety of foods that went well beyond mere survival, although they were obviously cooked by simpler methods. Barnyard animals were raised, such as hens that gave eggs, and sheep that gave milk to be made into cheese. Cereals were grown (the most common were the barley and millet used to make a kind of "focaccia", or flat loaf, still found today in Garfagnana and called **migliaccio**) and legumes such as broad beans, chickpeas and **fagioli dall'occhio** – black-eyed peas – while the other varieties, the basis for many Tuscan dishes of today, were to arrive only with the discovery of America. Legumes were the basic ingredient of nutritious soups and porridges.

Among the dishes that very probably originated from these two civilizations and that have persisted down to our own day, albeit with different ingredients and cooking methods, are those that can be considered the ancestors of dishes such **crostini di fegatini di pollo** – chicken livers, a crucial ingredient of many other recipes as well, such as **brodo con le cicche** – and **buristo** from Lucca – of ancient Greek derivation, this kind of charcuterie was eaten by the Romans in honor of Faun, a god of fertility – the **testaroli** made of "farro" flour from Luni, **semolino fritto** and the preparation of **dolceforte**, an elaborate sauce with a contrasting sweet-salty taste that reached its peak of success in Medieval-Renaissance times and was used mainly as accompaniment to meat dishes (hare and wild boar cooked in this way are great delicacies today) and the **schiacciata con l'uva** typical of the Florence area. Always and everywhere, great importance was given to wine, whose primordial production began at that time, and which was frequently drunk mixed with honey.

Tuscan Cooking from the Renaissance to the 20th Century

With the barbarian invasions, Tuscan gastronomy experienced a long period of decline, in which raw materials became scarce. The varieties and quantities of foodstuffs declined, and for housewives it became a problem to find something to put in the pot for every day. The foods available were for the most part legumes, onions, eggs and, in the best of cases, chicken. It was at this time that dishes made of scraps and leftovers originated, such as **ribollita**, **panzanella** (the version with tomatoes appeared only with the discovery of America) and **trippa**.

Furthermore, cooking was influenced by the Christian religion, which preached parsimony and frugality, although subsequently convents and monasteries almost always had an abundance of foods, especially on great occasions such as patron saint's days and public festivals. And more and more pilgrims passing through Tuscany on their way to Rome brought their own cooking traditions (still remaining today is **zuppa longobarda** or **lombarda**, typical of the Valdelsa). Foods considered pagan were prohibited. The production and consumption of pork increased; it was easier to preserve under salt, an element deemed so precious that it was used as wages, or 'salary'. But this is also the period during which the Florentines began to bake "sciocco" (literally, silly) bread, that is salt-free, in response to the blocking of the ports essential for trading by their rivals the Pisans. Even the crusades to the Holy Land contributed to development, bringing knowledge of new ingredients and the contamination of Oriental cooking. It is in fact thought that the **ricciarelli** of Siena, made with almonds, were invented during this period.

In these years there originated such dishes as **fette col cavolo nero**, **pattona** made of chestnut flour, the different kinds of **farinate** (of chickpeas or chestnuts), the **frittate con cipolle** (the best onions are still those grown at Certaldo) and sweets such as the **panforte** of Siena and the **brigidino** of Lamporecchio. Delicious recipes even today, although containing different ingredients (for example, spices and saffron were widely used to flavor meat dishes).

The most notable revival occurred however from the Renaissance on, with the increase in the spice trade with the Orient, but also with the discover of the American continent, which favored the exchange of produces and ideas and from which arrived not only tomatoes but also cornmeal, beans, turkeys, and later cocoa. The wealth of a household was judged by its ability to offer its guests the greatest number of dishes cooked with precious spices, and not

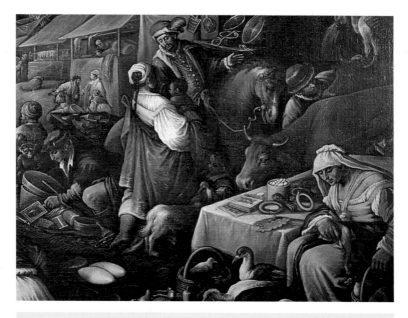

LEANDRO BASSANO (school of), *Market Scene*. Florence, Villa Medicea della Petraia (detail)

infrequently the great Tuscan families, the Florentines and Sienese in particular, grew rich expressly by trading in pepper and spices of all kinds.

The great lords and the courts looked upon dining as a moment of well-being for the mind and the body, but also as the occasion to establish powerful alliances. Dinners became real theatrical performances, with stupefying scenographic settings. Banquets now began to be held with costly, refined tablecloths, exaggerated amounts of food and splendid dishes – thanks also to the use of icehouses for the conservation of the most perishable foods and of wine – as well as artistic table decorations specially designed by famous artists. It is told, in fact, that Bernardo Buontalenti, who lived in the 16th-17th century, was one of the architects who specialized in these decorative arrangements. He is also said to have invented ice cream, and to have molded with it and with sugar extravagant decorations to embellish the most important festivities.

Emblematic of the splendor of the times were wedding banquets, such as that of Lorenzo de' Medici, known as the Magnificent, and Clarice Orsini, which took place in 1469 in Palazzo Medici Riccardi, lasted three days and had such an abundance of food that the bridegroom donated to his people 150 calves and 4000 dishes of hen, fish and game, all accompanied by wine, and it is said that hundreds of pounds of sweets and candies were consumed, while Donatello's statue of *David* stood at the center of the courtyard amid the splendidly adorned tables. But the Magnificent was not the only member of the Medici family to love good food. The great Catherine too, who married the King of France – to whom she brought as a wedding gift a sack of Tuscan beans – was

PIETER BRUEGHEL *Carnival in a Peasant's Home.* Florence, Museo Stibbert

known to be an excellent cook and an ardent gourmet who summoned to her court, where she also introduced the usage of the fork, Tuscan cooks and pastry-makers destined to leave a decisive imprint on the cuisine of France. Among the sovereign's favorite dishes, which have come down to us with some modifications, were **papero al melarancio** (our own version of the French duck with orange sauce), **cibreo**, the onion soup (called **carabaccia** in Florence, and **cipollata** in Siena), meat cooked in **dolceforte**, the sauce called **besciamella** and the **crespelle alla fiorentina**. Catherine is also known to have been greedy not only of artichokes, especially in **pinzimonio** (which she consumed to the point of indigestion, convinced of their aphrodisiacal power), but also of the sweet called **zuccotto** and of **sorbetto**, created according to legend by a butcher, the winner of a cooking competition (still today a worldwide wine and food competition is held, dedicated to the powerful sovereign) by the Queen and, for his great skill, 'invited' to follow her to Paris. It was also at this time that there originated what were to become typical dishes of Tuscan cooking, such as **peposo**, said to have been invented by Brunelleschi (but still without potatoes and tomatoes), the pork roast called **arista**, sweets such as **schiacciata alla fiorentina** and liqueurs such as the Florentine **Alkermes**.

A very strong influence came from the cooking of other religions such as the Jewish faith, which thanks to its numerous communities in cities such as Florence, Livorno and Pitigliano (Province of Grosseto) introduced and added its culture to Tuscan foods (for example, with sweets such as the **sfratto** of Pitigliano and the **roschette** of Livorno). In the 17th century notable commercial expansion brought to Tuscan kitchens foreign dishes that began to adulterate the tradition, especially in the larger cities. Chocolate became the height of fashion, widely used as a beverage or in the preparation of dishes such as wild boar in sweet-and-sour sauce. In the 19th century, under the domination of Napoleon, a strong influence came from French cuisine, leaving traces in the typical dishes of the Island of Elba, such as **spigola all'imperiale**.

With the Unification of Italy and Florence as its capital (1865-1870), traditional cooking was relegated to the outlying district, in favor of French cuisine, with sumptuous banquets 'in the French manner', reserved to the wealthier classes, especially in the Tuscan administrative center of Florence (except during festivals such as Carnival, in which all pleasures were conceded, *in primis* that of the palate, even for the common people).

In the early 20th century and between the two World Wars, a period of greater poverty and austerity returned. On the tables of the nobility, the seasonal foods grown on the farms they owned were served, while great dishes were restricted to solemn occasions such as weddings, diplomatic dinners and grand balls; and ordinary citizens cooked even more simply, usually consuming only one meal a day. The only luxury, for those who could afford it, was a meat dish as the main course for Sunday dinner.

MAXIMILIAN PFEILER, *Fruit and Crystals*, Rome, Palazzo di Montecitorio (detail)

Tuscan Cooking Today

It is known that the character of a people is revealed by their cooking and even though tastes have had to adapt to new demands, those of tourists and otherwise, Tuscan cooking today has rediscovered the ancient tradition, with the aim of exalting and enhancing flavors that are genuine, simple and straightforward. Everywhere restaurants will offer ancient recipes in their daily fare, such as soups, tortelli, roasts, fried dishes, cakes and many others. Each dish, even when made of few ingredients, is exalted and refined by the use of aromatic herbs, among them garlic, onions, very often rosemary, sage, basil, bay leaves, parsley, juniper berries, anise, as well as spices such as nutmeg, cloves, cinnamon and pepper. As this is a land of great peasant tradition, it is a must to sample what the land offers in addition to the excellent local products such as cheeses, charcuterie and wines; while along the coast and on the islands, fish is widely used in many dishes. And it will not be hard to find, especially in Maremma and Casentino, dishes based on game and recipes enriched with truffles and porcini mushrooms. For centuries the city of Florence has predominated in the cooking of the region, and frequently it is associated with

dishes and delicacies as if they had originated in its territory, but this is only a question of practicality and tourist renown, since the vast field of Tuscan cooking is not limited to steak or "ribollita": each city, town and village has its own variation or its own characteristic dish that is well worth sampling. The best-known dishes to be sampled in "trattorie" are listed below, with the advance notice that the vast nature of the subject has imposed limitation on the number. The various sections dedicated to the cities will contain mention of the typical recipes of the area and suggestions as to restaurants where they can be tasted, although we strongly advise you to explore and discover them for yourself. We will describe the traditional dishes handed down by grandmothers, mothers, expert chefs and amateur cooks, we will give the best known recipes and those simplest to make at home with variations even more modern; and for some of them, we will recount the curious facts of their origin and historical usage. We intend to, and we can, give only a panoramic view, remaining suspended between tradition and innovation, in a commingling of savors that has no equal in any other Italian region.

WINE

Wine would rightly call for a long chapter of its own. The typical straw-covered flask of Chianti with the symbol of the "Gallo Nero" (Black Rooster) is known the world over. Tuscany has been, in fact, since the time of the Etruscans, one of the most prestigious Italian zones for wine production and today the exportation of wine constitutes one of the major sources of its economy. Every year, moreover, its wines are awarded prizes in competitions held all over the world, and are always present in the most important classifications of the sector.

In the Middle Ages, wine was produced in every part of the region, and already at that time the wealthier families were marketing, in addition to precious fabrics and spices, the wine and often the olive oil produced on their estates outside the city, selling them in the typical "buchette", the niches in the walls of building still to be seen around Florence. And it was with red wine that they cooked, before the arrival of the tomato.

Starting in the 15th century, the production of Chianti was governed by precise procedures dictated by the "Chianti League"; in the 18th century, it had become so important that a decree was issued to protect its name and its adulteration and contraband were prohibited. Tuscan wine however is not only that of the Chianti area, which stretches between the provinces of Florence and Siena; in every part of the region excellent wines are produced, each with its own characteristics, depending on the manifold factors that determine its quality, which is however always high. Today, in any case, wine production is predominantly controlled by the most important families of Tuscany, who have transformed their farms into well-organized companies. This is the case, for example, of the Frescobaldi family (owners of vineyards also outside of the region and outside of Italy), of the Ricasoli, the Antinori and the Corsini, to mention only a few. In recent years, wine tourism has received strong impetus, thanks also to the willingness of olive oil and wine producers to open their cellars at some times of the year – usually in May and again in August, in September for the grape harvest and in November to sample the "vino novello" (new wine) – for wine-tasting and to explain the procedure followed to arrive at the finished product. Furthermore, panoramic wine tours are now offered along the 14 routes of the "Strade del Vino" (Wine Routes) scattered throughout the territory, with stops made here and there to sample a good glass of wine.

Among the many labels found here are: **Chianti Classico** – with the other sub-zones denominated **Colli Senesi**, **Colli Aretini, Colline Pisani**, **Colli Fiorentini**, **Montalbano**, **Rufina** – **Barco Reale di Carmignano**, **Aleatico dell'Elba** and so on, up to the noblest and most famous **Morellino di Scansano**, **Bolgheri Sassicaia, Solaia, Tignanello** and **Brunello di Montalcino,** all of them mainly red in color (either light or dark) and with a dry savor that perfectly accompanies meat and charcuterie, vegetable dishes and many soups. Each of these wines is produced according to strict rules that confer on it the denomination of DOC or DOCG. White and rosé wines too have an important place on the tables of all the world, among them **Vernaccia di San Gimignano**, **Bianco di Pitigliano**, those of the **Val di Cornia,** and the recent **Rosado di Toscana Igt,** excellent with white meats and fish, and truly special with numerous kinds of cheese. As dessert then, it is almost compulsory to ask for **biscotti di Prato** (crunchy cookies containing almonds) and a good glass of **Vin Santo** made of selected white grapes left to wither on the vine; it is generally amber yellow in color, and can be either sweet or dry. Its production is very ancient – it is thought to have been used for the first Masses celebrated in Christianity – and around its name have grown up curious legends. One of the best known is that of the Franciscan monk from Siena who, during an epidemic of the plague in the 14th century, treated the victims of the disease with the wine used for the Mass, which appears to have had miraculous powers, from which derives its name. The other story is linked to the Ecumenical Council held in Florence in 1439. During a dinner, the Greek representative, upon tasting the wine, exclaimed "Xantos", mistaking it for the wine produced in his own country. Those around him heard the word instead as "Santo" (holy) and since then that has been its name.

For some years now, a new way of tasting wine has come into vogue, with the production of jellies made of the most famous labels, that are a good accompaniment to cheeses, boiled meat, simple hard-boiled eggs as well as toast with melted cheese or Colonnata lard, **crostini** with liver paste and charcuterie. Among the very special ones are the jellies made of wines such as Morellino di Scansano, Brunello di Montalcino, Barco Reale, Carmignano, Ghiaie della Furba and Vin Santo.

The Wine Routes

1. *Colli di Candia and Lunigiana* (wines: Candia dei Colli Apuani Secco, Amabile or Abboccato and Vin Santo; Colli di Luni Bianco, Vermentino or Rosso).

2. *Colline Lucchesi and Montecarlo* (wines: Rosso, Merlot, Sangiovese, Bianco, Sauvignon, Vermentino, Vin Santo and Vin Santo Occhio di Pernice).

3. *Chianti Rufina and Pomino* (wines: Chianti Rufina).

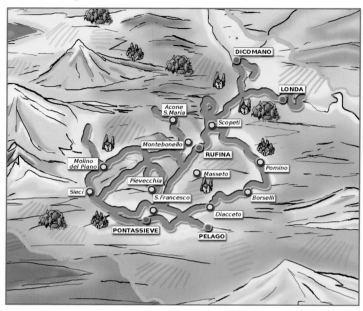

4. *Medicea dei Vini di Carmignano* (wines: Barco Reale di Carmignano; Barco Reale Rosato; Vin Santo di Carmignano and Vin Santo di Carmignano Occhio di Pernice).

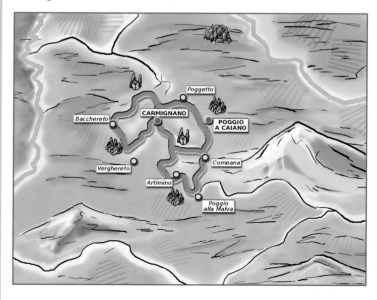

5. *Colline Pisane* (wines: Chianti delle Colline Pisane; Bianco di S. Torpé; Colli dell'Etruria Centrale; Montescudaio Bianco, Rosso and Vin Santo).

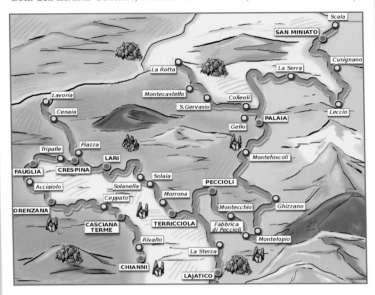

6. *Chianti Colli Fiorentini* (wines: Bianco and Vin Santo Empolesi; Colli dell'Etruria Centrale Rosso, Bianco, Novello and Vin Santo; Pomino Bianco and Rosso).

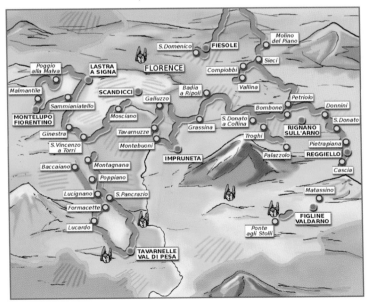

7. *Montespertoli* (wines: Chianti di Montespertoli).

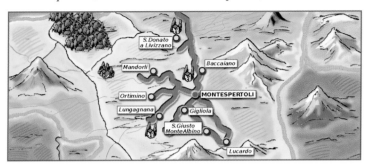

8. *Vernaccia di San Gimignano* (wines: Brunello di Montalcino; Vernaccia di San Gimignano; Chianti dei Colli Senesi; Moscatello di Montalcino; Orcia Rosso and Bianco; Rosso di Montalcino; Sant'Antimo; Vin Santo del Chianti Classico).

9. *Nobile di Montepulciano* (wines: Vino Nobile di Montepulciano; Rosso di Montepulciano; Val d'Arbia; Vin Santo di Montepulciano).

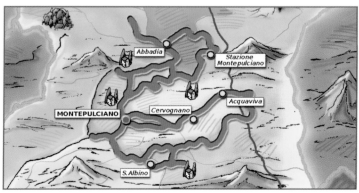

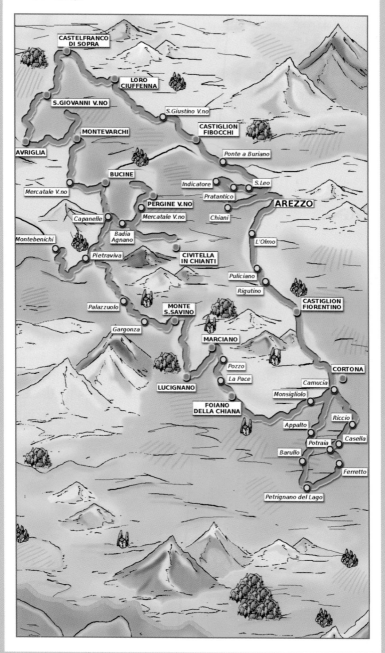

10. *Terre di Arezzo* (wines: Chianti dei Colli Aretini; Cortona; Valdichiana).

11. *Costa degli Etruschi* (wines: Bolgheri Bianco, Vermentino, Rosato, Rosso and Vin Santo; Elba Bianco, Rosso, Rosato, Ansonica, Ansonica Passito, Vin Santo, Vin Santo Occhio di Pernice, Aleatico and Moscato; Val di Cornia Bianco, Vermentino, Rosato, Rosso, Ansonica, Ansonica and Aleatico Passito, Suvereto).

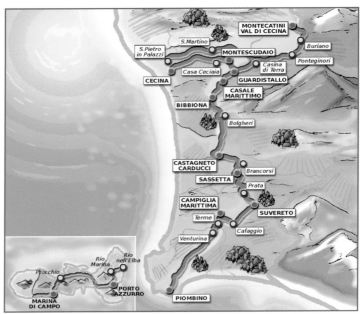

12. *Monteregio di Massa Marittima* (wines: Monteregio di Massa Marittima Rosso, Rosso Riserva, Novello, Rosato, Bianco, Vermentino and Vin Santo).

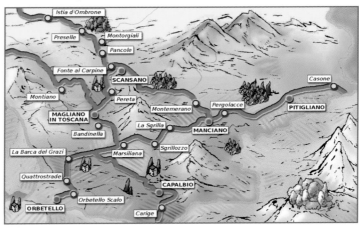

13. *Montecucco* (wines: Montecucco Rosso, Bianco, Vermentino).

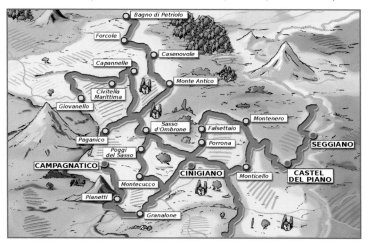

14. *Colli di Maremma* (wines: Bianco di Pitigliano; Morellino di Scansano; Parrina Rosso, Rosso Riserva, Rosato and Bianco; Sovana; Capalbio Rosso, Bianco, Sangiovese, Vermentino and Vin Santo; Ansonica).

PORK PRODUCTS

The slaughtering of the pig, in wintertime, was a real festival for the farmers, who gathered for the occasion to celebrate the "smigliacciata", where the table was loaded with a triumph of dishes based on pork: from the many kinds of soup made with the scraps, to sausages, "ciccioli" and pork liver wrapped in membranes, to the pork roast called "arista", to pork chops with winter cabbage or turnips, down to black puddings and blood sausages; for one whole day, there was no other thought than sitting at table and enjoying the feast. From this ancient appointment, a rich array of charcuterie, the boast of the region, has remained. In the Sienese hill country there has recently come back into vogue the breeding, in the semi-wild state, of a particular breed of pigs, the so-called **Cinta Senese**, named for its "cinta", the belt of light-colored hair that runs around its body. The charcuterie made from this special breed is very savory, thanks also to its diet, which consists of acorns, tubers, cereals and truffles.

Capocollo or **coppa** – Delicately flavored charcuterie made from part of the pig's neck, marinated in Chianti wine and spices and left to season.

Finocchiona – This large, soft sausage aged for one year originated in the Florentine area, but by now its production, which follows an ancient procedure, is common to other parts of the region as well, so that it is found everywhere. It owes its name to the fennel ("finocchio" in Italian), preferably wild for its antiseptic properties, contained in the mixture – made with the noblest, leanest cuts of pork – to which are added pepper, garlic and a little red wine. Excellent with bread, it is ideal with fresh broad beans. In the Province of Florence an even softer version is produced, called "sbriciolona" (crumbling) because as it is sliced, strictly by hand, it crumbles slightly.

Lardo di Colonnata – A kind of charcuterie of rosy white color, very fragrant (it contains many spices such as pepper, cinnamon, cloves, coriander, sage and rosemary), made of lard seasoned for at least six months in marble basins rubbed with garlic, according to a particular procedure of ancient tradition. Typical of the Alpi Apuane mountainous area, it is widely used in Tuscan cooking, thanks to its delicate flavor, in dishes ranging from starters to main courses; used to heighten the flavor of roasts, to soften fillings and, when diced, it is excellent sautéed in a pan and added to salad, or even in unusual combinations with skewered pieces of fish. But to experience its true softness and tasty flavor, it should be cut very fine and placed on warm slices of Tuscan bread, where the heat makes it dissolve a little.

Pancetta arrotolata – The fatty pigskin is rolled up, flavored inside with spices and aromatic herbs and covered with salt. It is perfect with cheeses, red wine and served on warm bread.

Prosciutto crudo – Cured ham produced mainly from pork of the Cinta Senese or the Casentino breed, seasoned with garlic, juniper berries, rosemary and pepper, and aged for 12-18 months. The meat, lean and very savory in taste, is best cut in slices; it is the perfect accompaniment to Tuscan salt-free bread. Among the most famous productions are those of Casentino, of the Cinta Senese and the Bazzone of Garfagnana.

Rigatino – Streaky bacon made with the fattest portions of the pig and flavored with black pepper and hot red pepper. It takes its name from the alternating "righe" (streaks) of lean and fat meat. Excellent on slices of toasted bread.

Salame – A very fragrant kind of sausage, flavored with spices, garlic and red wine, fine-grained and compact, seasoned for either a brief or a long time. It is still produced according to an age-old procedure.

Salame al vino – A kind of sausage that is still made today following an ancient recipe. Of fine-grained consistency, it contains coarser bits of fat. It is flavored with Chianti wine and has a medium seasoning time. It is frequently utilized in the preparation of other dishes (sauces, fillings).

Salsiccia – Long in shape, red in color, it has the soft consistency of selected lean meats, flavored with spices, aromatic herbs and garlic; it can be eaten raw, both fresh and seasoned.

Soprassata – Made by long boiling of the less noble parts and scraps of pork, coarsely chopped. The mixture is left to cool after having been covered with spices (hot red pepper, nutmeg, black pepper, etc.), lemon rind and salt. It should be tasted fresh on bread or in a salad with raw vegetables (carrots, celery and fennel). Its name derives from the fact that the sausage mixture is "soprassato", that is, compressed between wooden boards in canvas bags.

CHEESES

Marzolino – A cheese made of sheep's milk (milked in the morning and in the evening) in various shapes, one of the region's most ancient (it seems to have existed already prior to the 16th century, and also to have been appreciated by Michelangelo), it is a white cheese with a white crust when seasoned for a short time – about two months – while the crust on the dry version is reddish, due to the use of tomatoes. Its name derives from the month in which it is produced. Although it is typical of the Chianti area, excellent versions are also produced in Mugello and around Montespertoli.

Pecorino – Made of fresh sheep's milk and produced in round cheeses about 7 in. in diameter. The outside is treated with olive oil, or pepper, or ashes, while the inside is white in color. It is aged for at least two months, leaving it with a pungent, decided taste. Excellent with charcuterie, but also with honey and dried fruit or jam (as was the custom

in the 18th century). Every part of the region has its own production, although the technique is similar for all of them.

Pecorino di fossa – Made according to the same procedure as traditional pecorino, but aged in very ancient pits ("fosse", in Italian, for which it is named) of tufa stone, where numerous cheeses are piled in layers. After aging, the cheese has a sharp, unique flavor.

Pecorino in foglia – Round cheeses about 6 in. in diameter, light yellow in color with a dark crust, with an intense flavor and fragrance deriving from the leaves (usually those of the walnut or fig) in which they are wrapped or placed for aging, which lasts at least three months.

Pecorino al tartufo – Made of sheep's milk and black or "blanquette" truffles, it is salted and oiled and then left to age for at least a month. It is light yellow both inside and outside, with bits of truffle emerging from the crust.

Ricotta – Preferably made of sheep's milk, it is white with a soft, velvety consistency. Delicate to the taste, to be eaten fresh, it is excellent when accompanied by jam or marmalade. As a snack it is good when used as filling for the salty, flat loaf called "schiacciata". It is also used as filling for tortelli or as the basic ingredient of sweets such as pie.

Raveggiolo – A cheese of ancient tradition to be eaten without aging, it is made of sheep and goat's milk – in Mugello with cow's milk as well – and shaped into little cheeses. Since the cheese is wrapped in rushes ("giunchi" in Italian), it is also known under the name of "giuncata". Without a crust, it is white in color, acidulous in flavor and soft like a pudding in consistency, although that of Mugello is more compact. It is eaten dressed with olive oil and a dusting of pepper. As dessert, it is sometimes sprinkled with unsweetened cocoa, or covered with honey or fig and grape jam.

GLOSSARY

Starters, side dishes and snacks

Acciughe marinate – An inexpensive dish consisting of boned anchovies, soaked in vinegar and then dressed with a mixture of chopped aromatic herbs and olive oil.

Antipasto toscano – A typical dish of the territory where Tuscan charcuterie reigns supreme, often accompanied by liver paste on toasted rounds of bread or by porcini mushrooms preserved in olive oil.

Ciccioli – A culinary specialty consisting of toasted scraps left over from pork processing, after the fat has been melted into lard. Salted, flavored with aromas and pressed, they have become a fashionable delicacy.

Crostini toscani – Another classic Tuscan "antipasto" (starter) consisting of a sort of fresh pâté of chicken livers and spleen, capers and anchovies spread on slices of toasted bread dipped in meat stock.

Crostone col cavolo nero – A typical starter consisting of a slice of Tuscan bread dressed with Tuscan olive oil rubbed with garlic and garnished with boiled winter cabbage, salt and pepper.

Fagioli all'uccelletto and **al fiasco** – A side dish consisting of boiled beans warmed over in olive oil, garlic and sage, with the addition of tomatoes. Beans cooked in a flask are instead usually cooked in a fireplace, near the fire, in a long-necked glass bottle.

Fettunta – A typical and very simple starter or snack consisting of slices of toasted Tuscan bread, rubbed with garlic and dribbled with olive oil.

Fritto di verdure – A mixture of seasonal vegetables (potatoes, artichokes, pumpkin and zucchini flowers, eggplant, etc.) fried in a light batter; surprisingly good are sage leaves fried in this way.

Insalata di fagioli e soprassata – An appetizing pair, either as starter or as side dish, consisting of diced soprassata and Cannellini beans boiled until just done and dressed with Tuscan olive oil.

Insalata di soprassata – A more summery dish made with cubed soprassata mixed with celery, carrots and fennel and dressed with a sprinkling of lemon juice and olive oil.

Panino con fichi e salame – A typical simple late-summer snack, a sandwich of home-style bread or salty "schiacciata" filled with figs and Tuscan salami.

Pattona – Simple polenta made of sweet chestnut flour, to be sampled either in its softer, creamier version, or harder, more compact one, with cream; or as accompaniment to roast meat.

Pinzimonio – A simple dish of raw vegetables, preferably seasonal ones, to be dipped in a mixture of olive oil, salt and pepper, with the optional addition of balsamic vinegar or lemon juice.

Pasta and soups

Insalata di farro – A summer salad consisting of boiled and cooled farro, topped with fresh seasonal vegetables, usually cherry tomatoes, cucumbers, spring onions and basil. The winter version is the excellent **minestra di farro**, a hot soup.

Panzanella – A very simple rustic dish, mainly summer, made of stale Tuscan bread that has been soaked in cold water, dressed with vinegar, fresh tomatoes, cucumbers, sweet onions, olive oil and fresh basil. It is served as either a starter or a first course, and there is also a variation with sweet onions. The origins of this dish are ancient; it descends in fact from the "pan lavato" (rinsed bread) mentioned by Boccaccio and used by country-women as a hangover remedy for their husbands.

Pappa al pomodoro – A soup made of stale Tuscan bread and tomato sauce boiled in stock. It is served hot with fresh olive oil and basil.

Pappardelle alla lepre o al cinghiale – Pasta similar to tagliatelle but thicker, dressed with a sauce made of wild boar or hare cooked in red wine and tomatoes.

Pasta e fagioli – A fragrant, savory, soup containing pasta and puréed Tuscan beans flavored with tomatoes.

Ribollita – A specialty originating in Siena but spread through all of the other provinces, it is a soup made of beans, winter cabbage (a typical variety of cabbage grown only in Tuscany), stale Tuscan bread and vegetables, cooked for hours the first time in a terracotta pot, and then reheated later and dressed with fresh olive oil. Its name comes from the countrywomen's habit of cooking great quantities of this soup, which was then "ribollito" (re-boiled) and eaten for several days.

Meat, fish, and side dishes

Anatra all'arancia – The modern version of the "papero al melarancio" of Sienese origin, introduced to the Medicean court by Sienese cooks, who then followed Catherine de' Medici to France. It calls for a duck to be cooked first in oil or butter and white wine, then in a sauce made of orange juice and strips of orange rind.

Bistecca alla fiorentina – Although its name might be misleading, this dish is typical of almost all of the territory. Excellent steaks can be eaten everywhere in Tuscany, always complying with precise rules, the first of them being that the meat must come from cattle of the Chianina breed.

Cinghiale stufato – A kind of stew made of wild boar's meat marinated for a long time in vinegar and various aromatic herbs and then simmered over low heat in red wine and tomatoes. Wild boar's meat is also the main ingredient of many other recipes found all over the region.

Fritto di paranza – Various kinds of small fish, fresh from the morning's catch, simply floured and fried in sizzling hot oil.

Fritto misto alla toscana – Pieces of meat of various kinds, from chicken to rabbit, dipped in batter and fried, often accompanied by fried vegetables.

Pollo alla diavola, alla cacciatora, fritto, allo spiedo, al mattone – Chicken has always reigned supreme in the menus of Tuscan tradition, although in the past it was restricted to feast days in the countryside; today it is served in a vast range of recipes.

Rosticciana – A tasty, hearty dish consisting of pork ribs roasted on a grill or over glowing charcoal.

Tagliata di manzo, pollo, vitello – One of the specialties of Tuscan restaurateurs, who suggest as alternative to the classic steak various kinds of grilled meat already "tagliata" (cut) on a base of "rucola", porcini mushrooms or flakes of parmigiano and balsamic vinegar.

Trippa alla toscana – Part of the stomach of cattle, boiled, cut into strips and plunged into a tomato sauce with rosemary, bacon and parmigiano. Each province has its own version.

Cakes, pies, cookies and liqueurs

Ballotta – Chestnuts boiled in their skins, at times with the addition of aromas such as sticks of cinnamon and bay leaves; while the roasted version is called **bruciata** or **caldarrosta**.

Buccellato – A kind of soft, sweet bread made of flour, eggs and sugar, typical of the Tuscan-Emilian Apennines. It requires long, slow preparation and is found in various forms, either ring-shaped or as a long, thin loaf. Among its different versions is that of Lunigiana, flavored with citrus fruits, and that of the Lucchesia, the area around Lucca, with anise and raisins.

Budino di riso – Sweets of cylindrical shape made of short pastry filled with cream of rice flavored with vanilla.

There is also a version with rice and raisins soaked in Vin Santo.

Castagnaccio – An autumn sweet of ancient mountain folk tradition, famous all over the territory and called by various names depending on the area, among them "migliaccio", "pattona", "baldino", "ghirighio", etc., made of very few ingredients: chestnut flour, olive oil, rosemary and pine nuts or walnuts. It is thin and flat, with the characteristic cracks on the surface, fragrant and soft to the taste. One of the many versions also calls for raisins and orange rind.

Cenci – Cookies made of very thinly rolled dough, often in the shape of a bow, cut in strips and fried, typical of Carnival time. The best known are those made in Florence, containing sugar, eggs and Vin Santo. In Livorno instead the recipe also calls for aniseed added to the dough.

Ciambellino – Cookies made of crisp dough from the Tuscan 'humble cooking' tradition, containing eggs and flour, ring-shaped with variations from one area to another, typical of Easter time.

Frittelle di S. Giuseppe – Sweet fritters made of rice, raisins and milk, flavored with citrus fruits and aromatized with heavy dessert wines, of the Passito type, or with sweet Vin Santo. They are usually made for St. Joseph's Day (March 19). They are also called by the following names: "sommomolo", "frisoli" and "frittelle di riso".

Panpepato – Sweet rolls containing dried fruit, unsweetened cocoa and chocolate, honey and wine with a pinch of pepper, from which comes their name. Those of Siena, the best known, are instead round and flat, with a surface sprinkled with pepper and spices.

GIUSEPPE MARIA VITELLI, *Cake Vendor* (c. 38), Florence, BNCF, Pal. 10.2.5.23

Recipes

Starters, snacks, savory pies and luncheon dishes

Acciughe marinate (Marinated anchovies)

Utensils: small bowl, ovenproof dish
Preparation time: 20 min. + 1 hr. marinating time
Ingredients for 6 persons:
– 1 lb. of fresh boned anchovies
– 1 large red onion
– 1 clove of garlic
– 2 bunches of fresh parsley
– white wine vinegar to taste
– olive oil

Preparation:
① Use already cleaned anchovies; otherwise, cut off the heads, remove the entrails and bones, keeping the two halves joined at the tail.
② Slice the onion and place the slices in a small bowl to marinate with a little of the white vinegar, to eliminate the strong smell.
③ Place the open anchovies in the ovenproof dish in layers. Cover each layer with the chopped parsley and garlic mixture. Drain the onion slices and place them on top.
④ Add enough vinegar to cover the fish. Cover and let marinate for one hour.
⑤ Drain off the vinegar and dress with olive oil.

This is a typical starter, which is also served on the Tyrrhenian coast, but can be easily found in Florence, where fresh fish arrives every day.
🍷 Val di Cornia Bianco, Montecucco, Vermentino

Pinzimonio (Raw vegetables dipped in olive oil)

Utensils: 1 salad bowl, 6 small individual bowls
Preparation time: 20 min.
Ingredients for 6 persons:
– fresh, tender vegetables (fennel, carrots, artichokes, celery, radishes, cherry tomatoes, and spring onions) in the quantities desired
– olive oil, preferably new
– pepper, salt, vinegar or lemon juice

Preparation:
① Clean and wash the vegetables.
② Mix well the olive oil, salt, pepper and vinegar (or lemon juice).
③ Cut the vegetables into pieces (fennel, carrots and artichokes) and place them in a salad bowl as centerpiece.
④ Distribute the dressing in the small individual bowls and serve.

This simple recipe is served before meals or after them, as was the custom in Renaissance times, where the pinzimonio of vegetables and fruit served to decorate the main serving trays and triumphed at the end of the banquet when the elements of which it was composed were dipped in the gravy of the leftover meat dishes. There is also a less traditional variation that includes apples and walnuts. The presence of fresh artichokes is fundamental, due to the digestive properties of the plant. The artichoke, of ancient and uncertain origin (perhaps Egyptian) was introduced into Tuscany with great success, and is still cultivated today around Empoli, Pisa and Grosseto.

🍷 Ansonica Costa dell'Argentario, Colline Lucchesi Vermentino

Crostini di fegato (Fresh liver pâté on toast)

Utensils: deep pan
Preparation time: 20 min.
Cooking time: 30 min.
Ingredients for 6 persons:
– 1 lb. of chicken livers
– 5 tablespoons of capers
– ¼ cup of butter

– 1 medium-sized onion
– 2-3 anchovy fillets preserved in oil
– olive oil, 1 clove of garlic
– 1 glass of Vin Santo or white wine
– 2 loaves of bread of the baguette type or Tuscan bread (approx. 1 lb.)
Preparation:

① Finely chop the onion and sauté it in olive oil in the deep pan. Add the finely chopped garlic and the chicken livers, well washed and cleaned, and cook over high heat.
② Add a little wine and let it evaporate.
③ When nearly done, add the capers, rinsed and squeezed, the filets of anchovies and the butter.
④ Pour the mixture into the blender and blend to the consistency of a soft but compact cream; if necessary, add a little more butter; keep warm.
⑤ Spread the warm mixture on slices of toasted bread and serve. The crostini may be garnished with parsley and a dusting of pepper.

For centuries, slices of bread were used as plates. They were toasted and dampened with stock before the meal. The food was placed on them and at the end of the meal they were eaten, soaked in sauces and oil. This custom probably gave origin to this recipe, of which many variations exist: some cooks complete the cooking with vegetable stock or red wine or brandy, others instead use stale toasted bread dipped first in broth, while still others use no butter, obtaining a very soft cream. There is also a version made with veal spleen, which is chopped more coarsely, and one with pork liver. Around Arezzo, crostini are made with the addition of chicken, an egg yolk and pickles. In Siena they are frequently served with slices of bread dipped first in dry Vin Santo. The choice is yours; and whatever it may be, these crostini together with charcuterie and cheeses are the classic "antipasto toscano" that you will find in trattorie and restaurants everywhere… but you will never eat it the same way twice.

🍷 S. Gimignano Rosso Novello, Montescudaio Bianco, Bolgheri Sauvignon

Crostone al cavolo nero (Toast with winter cabbage)

Utensils: deep pot, oven grill, frying pan
Preparation time: 20 min.
Cooking time: 3-5 min. for the bread; 20 min. for the winter cabbage

Ingredients for 4 persons:
– 4 slices of stale Tuscan bread about ½ in. thick
– 2 lb. of winter cabbage
– 2 cloves of garlic
– olive oil, salt and black pepper or hot red pepper

Preparation:
① Clean the winter cabbage and parboil it in a pot with salted water for about 20 min.
② Toast the slices of bread under the grill and rub them with garlic on both sides.
③ Drain, squeeze dry and chop the winter cabbage.
④ Heat the olive oil in a pan, sauté the cabbage for a few minutes and salt it.
⑤ Serve the cabbage on the slices of toasted bread, dressing it with abundant olive oil and a sprinkling of black pepper or hot red pepper.

To enrich this dish, a spoonful of boiled "Zolfini" beans can be added to each slice of toast, or the toast can be flavored with slices of Colonnata lard placed on the toasted bread rubbed with garlic. The slices are then put in the oven for 5 min. to dissolve the lard before adding the winter cabbage.

🍷 Bolgheri Rosso, young Chianti, Rosato di Carmignano

Fettunta (Toast with olive oil)

Utensils: oven grill or a pan
Preparation time: 10 min.
Cooking time: 10 min.
Ingredients for 6 persons:
– 6 slices of stale Tuscan bread
– 1 clove of garlic
– olive oil, salt and pepper to taste
Preparation:
① Heat the grill well.
② Toast the slices of bread under the grill, turning them to toast both sides.
③ When they are crunchy, remove them from the oven and rub them well with garlic.
④ Sprinkle with salt and pepper and dress with abundant olive oil.

The slices of toasted bread can be accompanied by cheese, such as "marzolino" or "pecorino toscano", and fresh broad beans.

🍷 Colli dell'Etruria Centrale Novello, Vernaccia di S. Gimignano

Pasta and soups

Minestra di farro (Farro soup)

Utensils: deep pot
Preparation time: 20 min.
Cooking time: 45 min.
Ingredients for 4 persons:
– 2 cups of farro from Garfagnana
– 1 lb. of winter cabbage
– 1 hambone
– 1 red onion
– 1 carrot
– 1 stalk of celery
– 2 cloves of garlic
– a few sprigs of parsley
– a few leaves of sage
– 8 cups of water
– 6 tablespoons of olive oil, salt, black pepper
– grated parmigiano or pecorino to taste

Preparation:

① Soak the farro in warm water, removing any spoiled grains.

② Sauté the finely chopped vegetables in olive oil for a few minutes, then add the farro, the salted water, ham bone, parsley and sage. Simmer for about 40 min. until the soup has thickened and the farro is done.

③ Serve with a dribbling of fresh olive oil, a sprinkling of pepper and a handful of grated parmigiano. You may accompany the soup with slices of toasted bread rubbed with garlic (optional).

A richer version calls for browning diced streaky bacon with the vegetables, and adding pearl barley, potatoes, lentils, Cannellini beans and black-eyed peas.

🍷 Colline Lucchesi Rosso, Carmignano Rosso

Panzanella (Bread salad)

Utensils: 2 bowls
Preparation time: 20 min.
Ingredients for 6 persons:
– 1 lb. of stale Tuscan bread (or other home-style type)
– 6 ripe tomatoes
– 2 mild red onions or a few spring onions
– fresh basil leaves
– a few tablespoons of red wine vinegar
– olive oil, salt and pepper to taste

Preparation:

① Tear the bread into pieces and place them in a bowl to soak in cold water. In the other bowl, cube the tomatoes and slice the onions fine.

② Take a little of the soaked bread at a time, squeeze it well, crumble it and add it to the tomatoes and onions.

③ Dress the ingredients with olive oil, salt, vinegar and basil leaves torn into bits.

④ Refrigerate the bread salad for at least 30 min. and serve it cold.

The origins of this typically summertime salad are ancient and humble. A descendent of the "pan lavato" (rinsed bread) mentioned by Boccaccio, it is also called "pan molle" (soaked bread). It was used, it seems, by the peasant women as a hangover remedy for their husbands. Its name may derive from the town of Panzano, in the Province of Florence, or from the term used for the bowl in which the bread was placed: "pane nella

zanella". Various versions exist, the most common being those of Florence and Arezzo, which call for the addition of cucumber and celery. In Chianti, a hardboiled eggs is also added, while in Livorno they add filets of anchovies, and in Viareggio, tuna fish and pickles. There has recently come into vogue a 'seafood' version, with the addition to the basic recipe of calamari and shrimp sautéed in a pan with garlic and herbs (thyme, sage and parsley). The only unbreakable rule concerns the bread to be used. For the best result it is preferable in fact to use salt-free bread of the home-style type, to ensure that the salad will not be sticky and too soft. The bread salad made in Garfagnana is one of the richest versions of this dish. Called Panzanella del Prete *(the priest's panzanella) it also calls for radishes, fennel, carrots, diced cooked ham and pecorino, tuna and anchovies preserved under oil, hard-boiled eggs, sweet peppers and capers.*

🍷 Vernaccia di San Gimignano, Capalbio Doc Vermentino

Pappa al pomodoro (Bread and tomato soup)

Utensils: large terrine (preferably terracotta)
Preparation time: 10 min. + 40 min. resting time
Cooking time: 20 min.
Ingredients for 6 persons:
– ¾ lb. of stale Tuscan bread sliced thin
– 1 lb. of ripe tomatoes, seeded, skinned and cut in pieces
– 1 crushed clove of garlic
– 4 cups of hot vegetable stock
– 5 tablespoons of olive oil
– a few leaves of fresh basil, salt and pepper

Preparation:
① Lightly brown the garlic in the olive oil over low heat for a few

minutes, then add the tomatoes cut in pieces, the bread, a little salt and a sprinkling of pepper.

② Raise the heat and cook for 5 min., then add the stock and bring to the boiling point. Simmer for another 5 min. from when it starts to boil. Remove from the heat, add the basil, cover and set aside to rest for 40 min.

③ Stir and mix well, then serve in individual soup plates with a dribbling of olive oil, a dusting of pepper and a basil leaf.

🍷 Montecarlo Rosso, Vernaccia di San Gimignano, Bolgheri Rosato

Pappardelle alle lepre (Pasta with hare sauce)

Utensils: deep pot, deep pan, wooden breadboard, wooden rolling pin
Preparation time: for the sauce 15 min. preparation of the meat; 40 min. preparation of the pasta + 30 min. drying time for the pasta
Cooking time: 20-25 min. for the meat, 10 min. for the pasta
Ingredients for sauce for 4 persons:
– ¾ lb. of lean hare's meat, preferably fresh and well hung
– interior organs of the hare (spleen and liver)
– 1 clove of garlic
– various herbs: rosemary, sage, parsley, bay leaves, hot red pepper
– ½ cup of strong red wine type Morellino di Scansano

– 1 cup of canned tomatoes
– olive oil, salt and pepper to taste

Preparation of the hare sauce:

① Finely chop together the interior organs and meat of the hare with the garlic, rosemary, bay leaves, parsley, sage and hot red pepper.

② In a pan, sauté the chopped mixture in olive oil; add the red wine and simmer over low heat until the cooking juices have evaporated.

③ Then add the tomatoes, salt to taste and continue to cook over moderate heat.

Ingredients for fresh egg pasta for 4 persons (about 1 lb.):
– 4 cups of flour
– 5 fresh eggs
– 1 tablespoon of olive oil, salt

Preparation of the fresh pasta:

① Pour the flour in a cone onto the breadboard; add the eggs, salt and a tablespoon of olive oil.

② Knead the ingredients together for about 10 min. or until the dough is soft and elastic and does not cling to the hands.

③ With a floured rolling pin, roll the dough to form disks, not too thin.

④ Sprinkle the disks of dough with flour to keep them from sticking. Leave them to dry on lightly floured trays, covered with clean kitchen towels, for about 30 min.

⑤ Fold the pasta a first time toward the center, so that the upper edges meet in the middle; fold it again toward the center and lastly bring the edges of the pieces together.

⑥ Cut the pasta into strips about ½ in. wide

Preparation of the dish:

① Cook the pasta "al dente" in abundant salted water, to which has been added 1 tablespoon of olive oil to keep it from sticking, for 4-5 min.

② Drain the pasta, add it to the pan containing the sauce and cook and stir for a few minutes.

③ Serve in individual bowls with a dusting of pepper.

To save time, you can use ¾ lb. of readymade dried "pappardelle" and can use rabbit instead of hare.

"Pappardelle" can be accompanied by many different kinds of sauce, ranging from porcini mushrooms to seafood. Those who like to experiment with new tastes should also try "pappardelle" with

cocoa, as well as the now classic versions with spinach and with chestnut flour.

🍷 Bolgheri Sassicaia, Carmignano, Brunello di Montalcino Riserva

Pasta e fagioli toscana (Tuscan bean soup)

Utensils: pot, deep pan
Preparation time: 30 min.
Cooking time: 45 min. for the dried beans; according to the type for the pasta
Ingredients for 4 persons:
– 2 lb. of Tuscan beans
– ¾ lb. of dried pappardelle or tagliatelle
– 4 oz. of bacon
– 1 can of tomatoes or 5-6 fresh, ripe, skinned tomatoes
– 3 crushed cloves of garlic
– 1 small onion or 1 scallion
– 1 dusting of hot red pepper
– 1 tablespoon of tomato paste
– 1 cup of olive oil
– salt and pepper to taste

Preparation:
① Cook the beans (when using dried beans, soak them overnight) for about 40 min.
② Finely chop the garlic and onion with the bacon.
③ In a pan, sauté the chopped mixture in olive oil. Add the hot red pepper, the tomatoes and lastly the tomato paste.
④ Pass the beans through a food mill back into their cooking water; bring them to the boil again, adding the tomato mixture.
⑤ Add the pasta to the pot and cook it along with the beans and tomatoes.
⑥ Serve dribbled with fresh olive oil.
🍷 Colline Lucchesi Sangiovese

Ribollita (Tuscan vegetable soup)

Utensils: large terracotta pot, large deep ovenproof pan
Preparation time: 40 min.
Cooking time: 2 hr.

Ingredients for 4/6 persons:
- ¾ lb. of green beans
- ½ lb. of pre-cooked Cannellini beans
- 1 lb. of beet greens
- 1 ¾ lb. of winter cabbage
- 1 medium-sized Savoy cabbage
- ¼ lb. of cubed streaky bacon
- 1 large red onion
- 1 leek
- 2 carrots

- 2 zucchini
- 2 stalks of celery
- 2 medium-sized ripe tomatoes, skinned and seeded
- 2 cloves of garlic
- 1 tablespoon of tomato paste
- 1 fresh (or powdered if preferred) hot red pepper
- a pinch of freshly ground black pepper
- 1 lb. of stale Tuscan bread cut in slices
- olive oil and salt to taste
- cold water

Preparation:
① In a terracotta pot, sauté the bacon and hot pepper in olive oil, then add the sliced onion, the carrots cut in rounds, the diced celery and the sliced leek; wither gently over low heat.

② Add the coarsely chopped winter cabbage and Savoy cabbage and let whither. Add the green beans, the sliced zucchini and the coarsely chopped beet greens.

③ Cook for 10 min., then add enough cold water to cover the vegetables.

④ Continue to cook; if the soup becomes too dry, add a little water.

⑤ When the soup is almost done, add the Cannellini beans, toast the slices of bread and rub them well with garlic. Place 2-3 layers of toasted bread in an oven pan, pouring the cooked vegetable mixture over each slice. Dribble with olive oil, sprinkle with salt and pepper and set aside until the bread has softened.

⑥ Mix well, heat in the oven for 10 min. and dribble with fresh olive oil just before serving.

🍷 Chianti, Rosso di Montalcino, San Gimignano Rosato

Meat, fish, and side dishes

Anatra all'arancia (Duck with orange sauce)

Utensils: casserole, potato peeler, saucepan
Preparation time: 30 min.
Cooking time: 70 min.
Ingredients for 4 persons:
– 1 duck (about 3 lb.) cleaned and trimmed of fat
– 3 oranges + 1 sliced fine for decoration
– 1 glass of white wine
– water as required
– 6 tablespoons of olive oil
– 1 sprig of rosemary, salt and black pepper

Preparation:
① Salt the inside of the duck and insert the rosemary. Place it in a casserole with the olive oil and brown it well all over for a few minutes, discarding the excess fat.

② Add the wine and half a glass of water and cover. Cook over low heat for 45 min.

③ Meanwhile, peel 1 orange with the potato peeler, discarding the bitter white part of the peel. Scald the strips of orange peel in the saucepan with a little boiling water for about 3 min., then drain and dry well.

④ Squeeze the oranges, add pepper, then 10 min. before removing from the heat, add the orange juice and strips of orange peel to the casserole containing the duck. Let the sauce reduce a little.

⑤ Serve the duck hot, cut in pieces, with slices of orange as decoration, and accompanied by mashed potatoes.

This dish can also be flavored with half a glass of orange liqueur ("Aurum" or "Grand Marnier") added along with the orange juice 10 min. before removing from the heat. In this case, use the juice of only 2 oranges.

🍷 Sparkling Bianco di Pitigliano

Fagioli all'uccelletto (Beans in tomato sauce)

Utensils: large deep pot, large pan (preferably terracotta)
Preparation time: 10 min.
Cooking time: 30 min.
Ingredients for 5 persons:
– 1 lb. of dried Cannellini beans (or 2 lb. of fresh ones)
– ⅔ lb. of fresh tomatoes, seeded and skinned (or 2 cups of puréed tomatoes)
– 3 cloves of garlic, unpeeled
– a few leaves of sage, 1 sprig of rosemary
– 1 fresh hot red pepper
– 7-8 tablespoons of olive oil, salt

Preparation:
① Soak the beans overnight in cold water (if dry), then cook them in a pot of salted water and set them aside in a little of their cooking water.

② In a saucepan, sauté the garlic with the sage and rosemary in olive oil for a few minutes, then add the tomatoes and hot red pepper and cook for 15 min.

③ Add the beans with their cooking water, salt and simmer over low heat to thicken the sauce for another 15 min.

④ Serve warm as a side dish with Florentine steak, or beef "tagliata".

A half a glass of dry white wine may be added together with the tomatoes.

🍷 Chianti

Pollo alla cacciatora (Chicken hunter's style)

Utensils: deep pan
Preparation time: 30 min.
Cooking time: 90 min.
Ingredients for 6 persons:
– 1 chicken (about 2 lb.)
– ½ cup of butter
– 1 ¼ cup of canned tomatoes
– 1 carrot
– 1 stalk of celery
– 1 onion
– 1 clove of garlic
– mixed herbs: juniper berries, bay leaves, rosemary, sage, thyme, etc.
– 3 tablespoons of olive oil
– ½ cup of dry red wine
– a few tablespoons of warm water
– salt and pepper
– a few sprigs of fresh parsley

Preparation:
① Clean the chicken well, pass it over a flame to eliminate the residue of feathers, rinse it, dry it and cut it into pieces. Do not remove the skin, to retain all of the flavor.
② Finely chop the vegetables and herbs and sauté them together in the pan with the olive oil and butter for about 5 min.
③ Add the chicken, salt, pepper and sauté on high heat for about 10 min. until the pieces are golden brown (pour off any excess fat) then add the wine and let it evaporate.
④ Add the tomatoes, skinned, seeded and cubed, and a few tablespoons of warm water. Simmer gently covered for one hour. Add a few tablespoons of water if the dish becomes too dry.
⑤ Serve hot garnished with parsley and accompanied by "fagioli all'uccelletto", mashed potatoes or polenta.

If desired, you can add 2 oz. of dried porcini mushrooms soaked for a few minutes in warm water, or ¼ lb. of fresh finely sliced champignon mushrooms. The same procedure can be followed with rabbit.

🍷 Chianti Classico, Chianti Rufina

Cakes, pies and cookies

Cantuccini all'anice (Anise cookies)

Utensils: breadboard, pan, oven paper
Preparation time: 30 min.
Cooking time: 40 min. in a moderate oven (350°F)
Ingredients for 8/10 persons:
– 5 eggs (3 yolks and 2 whole eggs)
– 1 ¾ cups of sugar
– 8 cups of flour
– 1 cup of softened butter cut in small pieces
– 1 grated lemon rind
– ¼ cup of "Sambuca"
– 1 teaspoon of aniseed
– 1 teaspoon of vanilla-flavored sugar
– 2 packets of baking powder

Preparation:
① Put the aniseed to soak in the "Sambuca". Sift the flour, form a hole at the center, add the ingredients gradually and mix well. Add the "Sambuca" with the aniseed only at the end.
② Mold the dough into 2-3 small loaves about ½ in. thick. Place them on the pan lined with oven paper and lightly buttered. Bake for 40 min. until the loaves are golden brown on top.
③ Remove them from the oven and cut them into slices about 1 in. thick. Let them cool; for even crunchier cookies, put them back in the oven again for a couple of minutes.

These cookies, very simple and very good, were the traditional breakfast baked by many grandmothers for their grandchildren.

Castagnaccio (Chestnut cake)

Utensils: terrine, wire whisk, round, low 9-10 in. round cake pan
Preparation time: 10 min.
Cooking time: 30 min. in a moderate oven (350°F)
Ingredients for 6/8 persons:
– 2 ½ cups of chestnut flour
– ½ cup of sultana raisins
– ⅓ cup of pine nuts
– 1 ¼ cups of water

– ½ cup of milk
– 6 tablespoons of olive oil
– 3 tablespoons of sugar
– 1 grated orange rind, 1 sprig of rosemary
– ¼ cup of Vin Santo
– 1 pinch of salt

Preparation:

① Soak the raisins in the Vin Santo for 15 min.

② In the terrine, mix the flour with the water and milk, 2 tablespoons of olive oil and the sugar, stirring well to keep lumps from forming, until the batter is smooth and rather fluid.

③ Add the well squeezed raisins, the pine nuts, the orange rind, and the pinch of salt; mix well.

④ Pour the mixture into a greased pan, dribble over it the rest of the olive oil, sprinkle it with the rosemary needles and more pine nuts, if desired.

⑤ Bake until the surface is covered with fine cracks.

⑥ Serve hot with whipped cream or fresh ricotta.

For a more compact consistency, let the batter rest in a covered bowl for 30 min. before pouring it into the cake pan. Legend has it that girls in love used to flavor this cake with rosemary needles, deemed a powerful love potion, before offering it to the young men, to make them fall at their feet.

🍷 Vin Santo del Chianti Occhio di Pernice Dolce

Frittelle di San Giuseppe (St. Joseph's Day fritters)

Utensils: terrine, 8 in. round frying pan, slotted spoon
Preparation time: 20 min.
Cooking time: 3 min. per fritter
Ingredients for 6 persons:
– 1 ⅓ cup of rice
– 6 cups of milk
– 5 tablespoons of Vin Santo
– 1 pinch of salt, 2 cups of flour type 00
– 3 tablespoons of sugar, sugar for garnishing
– 6 egg yolks + 2 egg whites
– 1 packet of baking powder
– 1 tablespoon of vanilla-flavored sugar
– 1 teaspoon of butter, 1 lemon rind
– sunflower seed oil for frying

Preparation:
① Cook the rice in the milk with the lemon rind (without the white part), the salt and the butter, until all of the liquid has dried. Remove from the heat and let cool.
② Place in the terrine the egg yolks with the Vin Santo, flour, sugar and baking powder.
③ Whip 2 egg whites and fold them evenly into the cream.
④ Heat the oil; when hot, drop tablespoonfuls of the mixture into it and fry them.
⑤ Remove the fritters with a slotted spoon, draining off the oil. Place them to dry on kitchen towels, then coat them with sugar.
⑥ Serve hot.

If desired, add ½ cup of raisins soaked in Vin Santo and a pinch of cinnamon.

🍷 Sparkling Bianco Vergine Valdichiana, Elba Aleatico Passito

AREZZO AT THE TABLE

The cuisine of Arezzo and its territory is both simple and rich in products linked to rural life and to the seasons, especially to the woods and fields distinctive of this area; and the lasting influence of its Etruscan origins can still be felt. Due to its geographic morphology, it has remained attached to tradition, little inclined to change and above all restrained in ingredients and vigilant of waste. At its base, and for Tuscan cooking in general, we find olive oil (a favorite dish around Arezzo is **zuppa frantoiana**, a soup whose ingredients include, in addition to wild herbs, fresh oil just come from the olive-mill), bread, potatoes (the Cetica potato is certified DOP) and cereals.

Highly important is the Casentino area, with its own culinary tradition made up of dishes, both sweet and savory, based on polenta (for centuries both that of cornmeal and that of chestnuts have been basic ingredients in 'poor' country cooking) as well as chestnuts, used to make not only bread but also porridges and soups, for which many tasty recipes have remained. Mushrooms, chestnuts and truffles are ingredients almost never missing from the table. The vast fields are perfectly suited to raising cattle of the "Chianina" breed, whose origin is thought to date from Etruscan times. This breed is famous the world over for their its meat (which also has the great advantage of not producing cholesterol) and in particular for its steak, so exceptional that even poems have been written in praise of it. And then there is the free-range 'Valdarno chicken', whose tasty though not especially tender flesh but is certainly worth sampling.

To begin with antipasto, we find the savory, aromatic prosciutto of Casentino, best when sliced by hand, the **sambudelli** – dried sausages containing a mixture of pork meat, spleen, blood, lungs and liver – and pecorino, or the so-called "abbucciato", a cheese whose characteristic rind darkens as it ages, with a scent of fields and meadows and a slightly bitter tang. Lovers of strong flavors should also sample **burischio**, a spiced sausage made of pork fat and blood, ingredients that, along with eggs and parmigiano, also form the basis for **migliaccio**. As a delicious snack, try **ciaccia fritta** – a kind of fried pizza made of water and flour – excellent with the charcuterie and cheeses of the area, or **brustichino**, a slice of bread toasted and dressed with olive oil.

Famous among the first courses are **gnocchi del Casentino** made of ricotta and spinach, ravioli filled with herbs and ricotta, **bringoli** – big spaghetti made by hand with flour and water – **tortelli** stuffed with potatoes and dressed with meat sauce, **pappardelle alla lepre**, **tagliatelle al tartufo** and excellent soups such as those of cabbage or farro. Another outstanding dish is the so-called **zuppa del Tarlati**, named for a powerful Arezzo bishop from the 14th century, a soup made of chicken and cream, showing the influence of French cuisine.

Outstanding among the main courses, in addition to steak and game (foremost among them hare and wild boar) are **centopelli**, **maiale con le mele**, **coniglio all'etrusca**, **pollo grillettato** cooked with lemon juice and aromatic herbs, pork liver conserved in fresh lard and **scottiglia** (in the Maremma and the Sienese territories it is called "buglione") – a stew of very ancient origin, exceptionally tasty, made with many kinds of meat – to be enriched with side dishes such as stuffed artichokes, fried celery, and beans cooked in a flask. Famous is the highly digestible Zolfino bean, small and round in shape, with its characteristic yellowish color, which is grown in the Pratomagno area; and then truffles and mushrooms of all varieties, including prugnoli, marzuolo and porcino, excellent either grilled or fried with a little fresh calamint.

Even far from the sea, the **baccaialata** made of salt cod is a good alternative to many meat dishes.

Noteworthy among the sweets are **baldino**, made of chestnut flour, as well as **pulenda dolce**, **torta margherita** and **frittelle dolci di riso**; and the cakes and cookies usually linked to religious festivities, such as **panina dolce** or **pangiallo**, soft in shape, with saffron, raisins and spices, **torcoli,** and the **ciaramiglia** cooked at Easter time. Nor should we forget **lattaiolo** – the ancestor of *crème caramel* – and the typical sweet of Arezzo, the **gattò aretino**, a roll of sweet dough with a chocolate cream filling.

The recommended wines are **Chianti dei Colli Aretini** and **Bianco Vergine di Valdichiana**.

GLOSSARY

Starters, snacks, savory pies and luncheon dishes

Brustichino – A slice of toasted bread, rubbed with garlic and dressed with olive oil.

Ciaccia coi friccioli – Savory, simple "schiacciata", a flat loaf made of leavened bread dough with bits of pork.

Pasta and soups

Bringoli – Long spaghetti, usually made of flour and water (there also exists a variation made with eggs) very similar to the *Pici* of Siena and Maremma. They are usually dressed with mushroom or meat sauce, and even have an autumn fair dedicated to them. In the Province of Siena they are called *Pici*.

Centopelli – A soup made of many kinds of meat (including tripe and bacon) cooked for hours in vegetable stock with cabbage, tomatoes and aromatic herbs.

Gnocchi del Casentino – These little balls of spinach, ricotta and cheese are usually eaten in broth, or browned in butter flavored with fresh sage and then covered with melted cheese.

Tortelli di patate – Pasta in the shape of square ravioli filled with potatoes, dressed with a simple tomato sauce or a meat sauce but excellent also with melted butter and fresh sage.

Zuppa del Tarlati – An unusual soup made of chicken, cream, vegetables and spices. This dish, based on French cooking, seems to have been introduced by the powerful Bishop Guido Tarlati upon returning from his voyage to Avignon. The Tarlati family is also mentioned by Dante and the famous bishop, a Ghibelline, was not only a man of the church (who is said to have celebrated Mass with a helmet and a shield on the altar) but also the lord of Arezzo, whose power extended as far as Città di Castello.

Zuppa frantoiana – An autumn soup made of wild herbs (wild fennel in particular) and fresh newly pressed olive oil.

Meat, fish, and side dishes

Baccaialata – A dish made of salt cod cut in strips, dressed with fresh tomatoes and chopped onion, carrots, garlic and celery, pepper, olive oil and parsley, and baked in the oven.

Fried celery – A tasty side dish consisting of celery fried in a batter of milk, eggs, flour and chopped fresh sage.

Scottiglia – A sort of winter stew made with a wide variety of meats cooked for hours in tomato sauce, for which no single recipe exists. Similar to the **buglione** found in southern Tuscany, between Siena and Grosseto.

Cakes, pies, cookies and liqueurs

Ciaramiglia – A leavened cake, typical of Easter time, made of sugar, flour and yeast flavored with anise soaked in Vin Santo and candied fruit.

Gattò aretino – A sweet in the shape of a roll formed of a layer of cake sprinkled with Alkermes on which is spread chocolate cream. It was the typical dessert served at country weddings. Its name derives from the French *gâteau*, while in the rest of the region it is known as "salame di cioccolato" (chocolate salami).

Lattaiolo – A thick cream whose ancient recipe calls for milk, sugar and eggs, flavored with nutmeg and cinnamon. The farmers used to bring it as a gift to the landowners on the feast of Corpus Domini.

Pulenda dolce – Among the many sweets based on chestnut flour, this is the simplest and tastiest, to be eaten with fresh ricotta mixed with sugar or sprinkled with cocoa.

Torcoli – Ring-shaped sweets containing flour, sugar, eggs, raisins, and pine nuts, flavored with anise and grated lemon rind.

Torta Margherita – A soft, fluffy, flavorful cake made of eggs, sugar, flour and pine nuts. The recipe of Anghiari (*see photo*) is famous.

Recipes

Pasta and soups

Gnocchi del Casentino (Gnocchi Casentino style)

Utensils: bowl, deep pot
Preparation time: 20 min.
Cooking time: 40-50 min. for the broth + 5 min. for the gnocchi
Ingredients for 4 persons:
– 1 ½ cups of fresh ricotta
– 1 lb. of spinach (also frozen)
– 2 eggs
– 5 tablespoons of flour
– abundant grated parmigiano
– nutmeg
– salt and pepper
Ingredients for the broth:
– a piece of lean meat
– 1 carrot
– 1 onion
– 1 stalk of celery

Preparation:
① Cook the broth in a pot and strain it when done.
② Boil the spinach in a little water if fresh, otherwise go on to the next step.
③ Put the spinach, cooked, squeezed and finely chopped, into a pan, adding the ricotta, the eggs, 4 tablespoons of parmigiano, 2 tablespoons of flour, salt, pepper and a pinch of nutmeg as flavor.
④ Work the mixture well until firm and compact; shape it into balls about the size of a walnut.
⑤ Bring the strained broth to a boil and drop the gnocchi into it one at a time; cook them for 5 min.
⑥ Serve in broth or, drained, with melted butter or meat sauce, always sprinkled with abundant parmigiano.
🍷 Chianti Rufina

Polenta gialla con cacio e pepe (Polenta with cheese and pepper)

Utensils: large, deep pot, ovenproof dish with cover or soup tureen
Preparation time: 20 min.
Cooking time: 45-60 min. + 10 min. resting time
Ingredients for 6 persons:
– 3 ½ cups of corn flour
– salted water for boiling (about 2 qt.)
– grated sharp pecorino (preferably made of goat's milk)
– pepper
– olive oil

Preparation:
① Heat the salted water; as soon as it comes to the boil, lower the heat and sprinkle the corn flour into it a little at a time it to keep it from forming lumps, stirring constantly for about 1 hr. to keep it from sticking. The polenta is ready when it detaches from the sides of the pot.
② Pour the polenta onto a breadboard and cut it in slices by the old method, using a string made of natural fiber (hemp, linen, etc.).
③ Place the slices in an ovenproof dish with cover, or in a soup tureen, dribbling them with olive oil and sprinkling with pepper and cheese. Continue in this way, forming layers.
④ Cover and place near a source of heat for 10 min.
⑤ Serve with an additional sprinkling of pepper.

Traditionally, this was a dish prepared during harvest time and throughout the autumn. The women brought it in big soup tureens to the vineyards to feed the hungry grape harvesters.

🍷 Colli dell'Etruria Centrale Novello

Zuppa frantoiana (Olive mill soup)

Utensils: large pan, slotted spoon, deep narrow pot
Preparation time: 30 min.
Cooking time: 20 min.
Ingredients for 4/6 persons:
– 4 cups of vegetable stock (soup cube permissible)
– 2 white onions
– 2 cloves of garlic

– 12 slices of Tuscan bread
– whole aromatic herbs (wild fennel, sage, rosemary, thyme, dried oregano, laurel) as desired
– a few ripe tomatoes
– salt, pepper
– fresh olive oil

Preparation:

① In the pan, sauté the sliced onions, peeled garlic and aromatic herbs for a few minutes.

② Scoop out the herbs with the slotted spoon and set aside.

③ Then place the slices of bread in the pan and brown them well in the olive oil. Drain off the excess oil and let them dry on paper towels.

④ In the deep pot, place a layer of bread, then some of the sautéed aromatic herbs, some pieces of peeled tomato, and then bread again, always finishing with a layer of bread.

⑤ Add just enough stock to cover; the slices of bread should remain crunchy.

⑥ Heat over a flame for a few minutes.

⑦ Serve in individual dishes with a sprinkling of pepper and a dribbling of fresh olive oil.

This is one of the many recipes for this soup, which is simple but very tasty. The other versions call for vegetables and legumes, but always dressed with fresh olive oil just come from the olive-press, the "frantoio" for which the dish is named.

🍷 Rosato di Carmignano, Colli dell'Etruria Centrale rosé, Pomino Bianco

Meat, fish, and side dishes

Maiale con le mele (Pork with apples)

Utensils: large, deep pan
Preparation time: 20 min.
Cooking time: 1 hr.
Ingredients for 6 persons:
– 2 lb. of pork (preferably neck muscle)
– 1 clove of garlic

– wild fennel or fennel seeds
– 2 cups of stock
– 5/6 small apples (Renette type)

Preparation:

① Cut the meat into pieces; brown them well in the terracotta pan with garlic, olive oil and wild fennel.

② When well browned, add the stock a little at a time and cook over low heat.

③ Wash the apples and cut them into four pieces, discarding the core but without peeling them.

④ Add them to the pork.

⑤ Cook gently so that the apples do not disintegrate: add pepper as desired and more fennel.

⑥ Serve hot accompanied by roast potatoes.

🍷 Sparkling Bianco Vergine Valdichiana, Chianti Colli Aretini

Scottiglia (Meat stew)

Utensils: 2 large, deep pots
Preparation time: 20 min.
Cooking time: 2 hr. and 30 min.
Ingredients for 6 persons:
– ½ lb. of beef muscle
– ½ lb. of rabbit
– ½ lb. of chicken
– ½ lb. of Guinea fowl or turkey
– ½ lb. of pork
– ½ lb. of lamb
– 2 cups of canned tomatoes
– pepper, olive oil, fresh sage, rosemary and hot red pepper (optional)
– 1 onion
– 1 carrot
– 1 stalk of celery
– 1 or 2 cloves of garlic
– 1 cup of red wine
– 1 cup of lightly salted water
– 6 slices of Tuscan bread
– 2 cups of stock if necessary

Preparation:
① Cut the meat in pieces and cook in a deep pot with 2 cups of water and a little salt for about 15 min.
② In another pan, sauté the chopped garlic, onion, carrot and celery in a little olive oil.
③ Add the meat, after having boned and peppered it; add the wine, a few leaves of fresh sage and a few rosemary needles and continue cooking.
④ Add the canned tomatoes, after having let the wine evaporate slowly; salt and cook for about 2 hr., adding more tomatoes if necessary and hot red pepper if desired.
⑤ Place the slices of toasted Tuscan bread in individual soup dishes, rubbed with garlic if desired, and pour the soup over them.

This is a very ancient dish from the Tuscan tradition that has many variations, such as the "buglione" of Maremma, and depending on what ingredients are available, known also as "cacciucco di carni" for the wide variety of meats used. The recipe given here is an abbreviated form, but equally flavorful and nutritious. In Casentino this meat 'soup' was a one-dish meal that shepherds and farmers used to make for neighborly meetings and to pass the time in the long winter evenings, telling stories or listening to the deeds of heroes sung by passing minstrels, the "cantastorie", and leaving the pot of meat to cook slowly over the fire, as if it had been forgotten. It was in fact the custom for each of the guests to bring any piece of meat he might have available at the moment, including scraps (chickens' necks, feet, etc.) to be cooked until it formed a tasty cream to be poured over slices of bread. The evening usually ended with glasses of wine and boiled chestnuts ("ballotte") or roasted chestnuts ("bruciate").

🍷 Carmignano, Chianti Colli Aretini Riserva

Sedano fritto (Fried celery)

Utensils: bowl, 2 frying pans
Preparation time: 20 min.
Cooking time: 30 min.
Ingredients for 4 persons:
– ½ lb. of fresh celery

– 1 oz. of butter
– ½ cup of milk at room temperature
– 1 egg at room temperature
– flour as needed
– a few leaves of fresh sage
– olive oil
– salt and pepper

Preparation:

① Clean and wash well the celery, then cook it in boiling water, removing it when half cooked. Cut it into pieces 2-3 in. long.

② Melt the butter in a pan; add the pieces of celery and sauté for 10 min.

③ Beat the eggs well in a bowl with a pinch of salt and pepper. Add the flour, sprinkling it to keep lumps from forming, the milk and the chopped sage; mix to a thick creamy consistency. Coat the pieces of celery with the batter and fry them in hot olive oil.

④ Serve hot as either appetizer or side dish.

🍷 Sparkling Bianco Vergine Valdichiana, Vernaccia di San Gimignano

Cakes, pies and cookies

Gattò aretino (Arezzo cake)

Utensils: bowl, 2 deep pans, rectangular oven pan
Preparation time: 20 min.
Cooking time: 15 min. in a moderate oven (350°F)
Ingredients for 6 persons:

– 5 eggs
– 1 ¼ cups of flour
– 1 ¼ cups of sugar
– 5 tablespoons of potato starch
– ¼ cup of butter
– ½ glass of Alkermes liqueur
– 1 packet of baking powder
– chocolate cream
– powdered sugar to decorate
– 1 pinch of salt

Ingredients for the "crema pasticcera":
- 3 ½ oz. of unsweetened chocolate
- 4 egg yolks
- ⅓ cup of flour
- ½ cup of sugar
- 1 pint of milk
- 1 stick of vanilla
- lemon rind

Preparation:

① Work the egg yolks with the sugar and beat the egg whites. Add the beaten egg whites, mixing gently with a wooden spoon from the bottom to the top to keep them fluffy.

② Melt the butter over hot water and add it to the mixture, stirring continuously, along with the flour, baking powder and pinch of salt, to form a soft, foamy cream.

③ Butter the oven pan and line it with a sheet of oiled paper; butter and flour the paper, removing the excess flour.

④ Pour the mixture into the pan, leveling the surface with a spatula. Place it in a pre-heated oven for 15 min. Do not open the oven door during this time.

⑤ To prepare the "crema pasticcera", bring the milk to a boil with the vanilla and the lemon rind, removing them as soon as the milk begins to boil.

⑥ Beat the egg yolks with the sugar in a pan. Add the sifted flour slowly to keep lumps from forming, then add the cooled milk.

⑦ Cook the cream over low heat, continuing to stir until it begins to boil.

⑧ In the meantime, melt the unsweetened chocolate over hot water. As soon as it has melted, add it to the cream mixture.

⑨ When the cake is done, gently detach it from the paper, place it on a breadboard and sprinkle it with the Alkermes diluted with a little water. Spread the surface with the cream and, with the aid of the paper, form it into a roll.

⑩ Garnish with the powdered sugar, slice and serve.

🍷 Sparkling Bianco Vergine Valdichiana

Torta Margherita di Anghiari (Anghiari white cake)

Utensils: terrine, 9 in. round cake pan
Preparation time: 30 min.
Cooking time: 45 min. in a moderate oven (350°F)
Ingredients for 6 persons:
– ⅔ cup of butter
– 5 eggs (4 yolks + 1 whole)
– ¾ cup of sugar
– 1 ½ cups of flour
– ½ cup of pine nuts
– grated rind of 1 lemon, preferably organically grown
– powdered sugar to garnish

Preparation:
① Melt the butter over hot water in a small pan on low heat. In the meantime, beat in a bowl with a wire whisk the sugar with 4 egg yolks and the whole egg, until it forms a soft, foamy cream.
② Grate into it the lemon rind (freeze the lemon rind before using, to grate it more easily).
③ Slowly add the sifted flour and the melted butter, stirring gently to keep lumps from forming.
④ Pour the cream into a buttered and floured cake pan. Level the surface with a spatula (preferably made of silicon) and sprinkle over it the pine nuts.
⑤ Bake in a preheated over for 45 min., without opening the oven door.
⑥ When done, let the cake cool, then sprinkle with the powdered sugar just before serving.

🍷 Chianti Colli Aretini Vin Santo Demi-sec

Lattaiolo (Milk pudding)

Utensils: bowl, pudding mold, large pan, large serving dish
Preparation time: 20 min.
Cooking time: 1 hr. in a low oven (300°F)
Ingredients for 6 persons:
– 4 cups of milk at room temperature
– ½ cup of sugar
– 6 eggs (1 per person)

– 1 piece of cinnamon
– 1 pinch of nutmeg
– 1 grated lemon rind
– 1 pinch of salt
– a little butter and some breadcrumbs to prepare the mould
– powdered sugar or cocoa to garnish

Preparation:

① Beat the eggs, then add the milk, the sugar, and all of the other ingredients, one at a time. Mix very well to obtain a smooth, creamy batter.

② Butter the mold and line it with the breadcrumbs, removing the excess. Then fill it with the cream.

③ Place the mold in a pan filled with enough water to cook it in the oven for an hour.

④ Unmold the dessert, turning it out onto the plate. Let it cool. Sprinkle with cocoa or powdered sugar and serve.

🍷 Chianti Occhio di Pernice Vin Santo, Chianti dei Colli Aretini Sweet

FLORENCE AT THE TABLE

Although the city of Florence needs no particular presentation to describe the treasures of art it offers the tourist, its vast province includes 44 communes scattered over a territory that stretches to the north as far as the Tuscan-Emilian Apennines, with picturesque towns such as Barberino, Scarperia, and Firenzuola; to the east with villages immersed in the verdant landscapes of the Casentine Forests Park, such as S. Godenzo; to the west with cities proper such as Empoli, Scandicci and big towns such as Montelupo (known for its artistic ceramics) and Certaldo – famous for its onions. And to the south, with big urban centers such as Pontassieve, Bagno a Ripoli and S. Casciano as far as the land of Chianti Classico with Greve and Impruneta, not to mention those towns that have now been encapsulated into the cities, such as Sesto Fiorentino and Campi Bisenzio. Like other parts of Tuscany, the province of Florence too has within it areas different from the city, the mountains and the countryside, which are not distinguished by their own individual culinary traditions. But here too, the dishes are made of simple, genuine ingredients, without considering the administrative center, whose cuisine has now been adulterated by external fashions and influences.

Florentine cooking can be identified with Tuscan cuisine in general, whose rules it has dictated, at least on the national level, and it is not hard to find in its restaurants many typically Tuscan dishes common to other cities in the region.

Olive oil reigns supreme in the dishes often accompanied by Tuscan home-style bread, strictly salt-free. The origin of this usage dates from the 12th century, when Florence and Pisa struggled for supremacy. The Pisans closed their ports to the Florentines for the salt trade, and they responded merely by baking bread that is "sciocco", without a grain of salt. Salt-free bread and vegetables form the basis of the **minestra di pane** (bread soup), which then usually becomes **ribollita** on the following day, with the addition of more vegetables and bread, and the basis of **pappa al pomodoro** and of the summer salad called **panzanella**.

Famous among the first courses are the **paste al sugo finto** – which are no other than macaroni or penne with tomato sauce – and the **penne strascicate** in sauce, and then **crespelle**, cannelloni filled with ricotta and spinach. Don't be frightened if a restaurant offers you **topini** (little mice) in all kinds of sauces. In Florence this is the name by which potato gnocchi are called. Potatoes are also used to make **tortelli mugellani**, to be accompanied with wild boar sauce, while the chestnuts of Casentino and Mugello are used to make tagliatelle, dressed with porcini mushrooms when in season, or with other ingredients.

During the winter months you can warm up with a good bowl of **carabaccia** – the onion soup beloved by the Medici family and Leonardo da Vinci – or of **zuppa longobarda**, another soup of ancient memory. Great space is reserved to meat of all kinds. First of all comes the famous **bistecca alla fiorentina** – the thick Florentine steak served by weight, cooked rare with a side dish of Cannellini beans dressed with olive oil or cooked **all'uccelletto**; followed by **peposo**, an ancient savory stew, roasted **arista di maiale**, **rosticciana** and **bardiccio** grilled over an open fire, veal **ossibuchi**, **pollo fritto** or cooked **al mattone** or **alla diavola**, by **lesso rifatto**, that is, left-over boiled beef, cooked again with the addition of other ingredients, by **anatra all'arancia** introduced by Siense cooks at the time of the Medici; without forgetting the variety meats used to prepare succulent dishes or snacks, as is the case of the ancient **cibreo**, of the **crostini di fegatini di pollo,** the **ciccioli**, the **trippa alla fiorentina** and the **panino con il lampredotto**, the **collo di papero ripieno** – in short, a triumph of recipes, all to be tried.

Vegetables are used to make such hearty dishes as the great **fritto misto**, which, if skillfully prepared, is highly digestible. Depending on which seasonal vegetables are available, its ingredients are never the same, and can include potatoes, zucchini and pumpkin flowers, artichokes, carrots, cauliflower and fresh sage leaves, which often accompany fried chicken, rabbit and lamb.

Sweets differ according to the season and are very simple, such as **schiacciata alla fiorentina** typical of Carnival time, along with **cenci**, a kind of cookie made with flour, eggs and sugar; **frittelle di S. Giuseppe,** fried sweets containing rice and raisins, the chocolate cookies called **quaresimali** and the **pan di ramerino**, a kind of bread with raisins and rosemary typical of Easter, and again during harvest time the **schiacciata con l'uva** made with bread dough to which are added black grapes and sugar. Typical of autumn is **castagnaccio,** a flat cake made of chestnut flour with pine nuts.

Delicious and available all year long are **bomboloni** made of fried dough, and **budini di riso**, as well as **torta al semolino** covered with melted chocolate, **torta della nonna**, filled with "crema pasticcera", and the **torta del nonno** version filled with cocoa-flavored cream.

Still today produced in Florence – the best is that of the *Officina Profumo-Farmaceutica di S. Maria Novella*, which follows the old eighteenth-century recipe – is the sweet liqueur **Alkermes** with its typical red color, widely used in pastry-making sprinkled over pies and cookies, as in **zuccotto**, a favorite dish of Catherine de' Medici, made of sponge cake, ricotta and cream, or **zuppa inglese** (English pudding), which is not exactly British, considering that it evolved from the Sienese "Zuppa del Duca".

As regards the production of wine, the Florentine territory forms part of the area of **Chianti Classico** and of the **Colli fiorentini**, with famous labels and typologies, such as those produced in the area of S. Casciano, Greve and Rufina. In the latter locality, a real *Museo della Vite e del Vino del Chianti Rufina* has been created.

In Florence the so-called "vinàini", picturesque wine-shops where the most famous Tuscan wines are sold by the glass, are well worth a stop. Among these, try the *Il vinaio* (Piazza del Grano, no. 10), *I Fratellini* (Via dei Cimatori, no. 38/r) or the *Fiaschetteria Nuvoli* (Piazza dell'Olio, no. 15).

GLOSSARY

Starters, snacks, savory pies and luncheon dishes

Coccolo – Balls of leavened bread dough, fried and salted; a variation of larger size is filled with charcuterie.

Covaccino – Thin, crunchy flat loaf made of bread dough baked in a wood-burning stove and dressed with olive oil and salt, an excellent accompaniment to charcuterie, but truly special with sweet toppings such as sugar or a hazelnut and cocoa spread such as Nutella®.

Crostone stracchino e salsiccia – A tasty starter consisting of Tuscan bread spread with stracchino, bits of sausage and pepper, browned in the oven. The same topping is often used for pizza.

Ficattola – Bread dough cut in diamond shapes and fried, to be eaten either topped with sugar or salty. Excellent accompanied by Tuscan charcuterie.

Panino con il lampredotto – A sandwich containing a very ancient dish beloved by the Florentines, consisting of the firmest, leanest part of beef stomach; its name derives from the lamprey fish, whose taste it vaguely recalls. Cooked in vegetable stock for hours, it is then cut into thin strips and put in a small bread loaf cut in half (the most commonly used is the "semelle", a soft, round loaf containing olive oil) which is first dipped for a few seconds in the broth in which the lampredotto has cooked, and flavored with pepper or, if preferred, with a green sauce made of parsley, capers and anchovies. Always to be accompanied by a good glassful of Chianti. These sandwiches are sold at the picturesque stands of the "trippai-lampredottai", one of the most fascinating, and at the same time retro trades, practiced outdoors on the vans equipped with big pots, glasses and sharp knives that have taken the place of the old wooden carts. In Florence, whether rain or shine, it is hard to miss the clusters of people of every kind, from laborers in overalls to bank managers in jacket and tie, leaning against the stands, lost in delight as they consume one of the cheapest, and at the same time most exclusive, snacks in the world. The best tripe sellers in the city are: *Palmiro Pinzauti* (Piazza de' Cimatori), *Mario Albergucci* (Piazzale di Porta Romana) and *Orazio Menzioni* (Loggia del Porcellino).

Pasta and soups

Carabaccia – A soup that was the height of fashion in the Renaissance, a favorite dish of Leonardo da Vinci, made of onions, and frequently eggs, in a tasty vegetable broth.

Originally the recipe was sweeter, since its ingredients included vinegar, almonds, cinnamon and sugar.

Cibreo – An ancient soup made of the interior organs of rabbit or chicken, along with the combs and wattles, mixed with beaten eggs.

Crespelle alla fiorentina – Cannelloni filled with spinach and ricotta baked in the over with white sauce and tomatoes. This dish was highly appreciated by Queen Catherine de' Medici, who introduced it to the French court.

Pasta al sugo scappato – A typical farmers' recipe ironically christened by the housewives with this name to indicate pasta dressed with poor sauce without meat, which was reserved to special occasions and so was also called "sugo di festa" (holiday sauce).

Penne strascicate – A tasty dish with a meat sauce cooked very slowly, to which the boiled pasta is added and "strascicata", that is, stirred well to let it absorb the flavor.

Risotto ai carciofi di Empoli – The city of Empoli is known for its production of artichokes, a vegetable beloved by Catherine de'Medici, who found them irresistible.

Here artichokes are combined with rice, to bring out their characteristic flavor at its finest.

Tagliatelle di farina di castagne – A hearty version of the more classic "tagliatelle all'uovo" made of appetizingly tasty chestnut flour. The dish can be dressed with either meat or vegetable sauces (try the menu with every dish containing chestnuts offered by the restaurant *La Bottega dei Gaudenti*, Castagneto di S. Godenzo, Province of Florence).

Topino – A smaller variation of potato gnocchi that lends itself to different kinds of dressing.

Tortelli di patate Mugellani – Produced for at least 250 years with the local potatoes of Mugello, these are soft, square ravioli with a filling of boiled potatoes and cheese. They are at their best dressed with beef sauce.

Zuppa longobarda – A soup dating from the time when the Lombard people moved down into the Valdelsa area, made of Cannellini beans, winter cabbage, herbs and stale bread.

Meat, fish, and side dishes

Arista alla fiorentina – Roast loin of pork on the bone, flavored with garlic, pepper, olive oil and rosemary. It is still cooked by the ancient recipe.

Baccalà alla fiorentina – One of the many ways in which salt cod is cooked in the region. Here the pieces of fish are first fried and then heated in tomato sauce.

Bardiccio – A sort of elongated sausage of beef or pork, soft, red in color, with an intense flavor of fennel, garlic and pepper. Excellent when grilled, often together with spare ribs, accompanied by Chianti Rufina, a wine from the Valdisieve area, which is also the place where "bardiccio" is produced. Many country fairs are dedicated to it in spring and summer.

Bistecca alla fiorentina – Although the name seems to pinpoint Florence as its origin, this dish is typical of almost the whole territory. The true steak, which comes from a young steer of the Chianina breed, consists of the T-bone with the filet and sirloin, and should not be too freshly butchered. It must be about 2 inches thick. Some prefer it cooked on a grill or over charcoal, after having let it marinate for a few minutes in olive oil, salt and pepper; others maintain that it should be dressed only when done (af-

ter having been cooked 5 min. on each side and 5 min. 'standing up', and still very rare), with a dribbling of olive oil, a sprinkling of freshly-ground pepper, a pinch of salt, and, if preferred, a little lemon juice. The name is said to derive from a group of English tourists who, having tasted and appreciated the slice of meat, called for a "bis" (encore) to the beefsteak.

Collo di papero ripieno – A very tasty dish consisting of ducks' necks filled with ground beef, grated parmigiano, eggs, soft bread, aromatic herbs and spices, cooked in stock. Usually served accompanied by vegetables preserved in vinegar and in olive oil. In the Mugello countryside, it was a dish typically served at Carnival time. There also exists a version with a filling made of duck and chicken liver.

Filetto di manzo – Filet of beef; this very tender cut of meat is often found on the menus of Florentine restaurants, dressed with a green pepper sauce or topped with a fresh porcino mushroom head and a twig of rosemary, in which case it is called "all'alpina" (Alpine style).

Inzimino – A sauce made of spinach or beet greens, garlic, parsley and tomatoes, generally used as dressing for calamari, cuttlefish and salt cod.

Lesso rifatto – Known also by the name of "francesina", this is a traditional country dish, consisting of leftover boiled meat (beef or veal) which is slowly cooked in a sauce of onions and tomatoes. Several variations exist, in some of which the meat is first sautéed with streaky bacon and red wine.

Ossibuchi alla fiorentina – A main dish consisting of a cut of veal with the characteristic 'eye', or hole in the bone. It is cooked in a sauce of tomatoes, herbs and wine, often used to dress pasta.

Peposo della fornacina – A dish of ancient tradition consisting of beef cooked with red wine and pepper. It is linked to the name of Brunelleschi, who is said to have invented it during the construction of the dome over the Cathedral, concerned that the "fornacini" assigned to control the fire for baking the tiles would have nourishment suitable for their night shifts at the furnaces. Accordingly, he created this dish abounding in spices, soaked in red wine and cooked for many hours over a low fire in terracotta pots, so that the meat would be tender and savory. After the discovery of America, the dish was enriched with such ingredients as tomatoes and potatoes, although the original recipe did not even call for olive oil.

Pollo alla diavola – A tasty recipe for cooking over the grill a chicken split in half and covered with aromatic herbs and a hearty dose of Cayenne pepper, accompanied by a sauce as hot as fire.

Trippa alla fiorentina – A recipe whose origin is lost in the night of time, which calls for tripe (veal or beef stomach) cut in thin strips and cooked in tomato sauce, served with butter and heaps of parmigiano. In another variation it is served cold with olive oil, salt, pepper and spring onions.

Cakes, pies, cookies and liqueurs

Alkermes – A sweet liqueur, bright red in color and highly aromatic. Produced already in the 13th century, it was drunk as a tonic, in the belief that it had the power to bestow long life. Today it is widely used in pastry-making to add color and flavor, and is even used by the Prato charcuterie-makers to color mortadella. The curious name comes from Arab and indicates the scarlet color of the cochineal insect, ground to make a powder used as an ingredient of the liqueur.

Bomboloni – Delicious sweets in the form of leavened balls of dough fried and either filled with cream, chocolate or jam or left open in the middle like a doughnut, powered with sugar. The best are those of *Cucciolo* (Via del Corso, no. 25/r).

Cenci – Sweets made of dough rolled very thin and cut into irregular strips (the origin of their name, which means rags), shaped like a bow and then fried, typical of Carnival time.

Pan di ramerino – A sweet, soft, leavened bread, produced since Medieval times, containing raisins and chopped rosemary (called "ramerino" in Tuscany) typically served around Easter. Although it is traditionally eaten on Holy Thursday, it can be found all year long.

Quaresimali – A specialty made of cookie dough with unsweetened chocolate shaped in the form of letters of the alphabet and flavored with orange, typical of the Lenten period. There also exists a variation made with chestnut flour and almonds.

Schiacciata alla fiorentina – A flat, rectangular cake, typical of Carnival, flavored with orange and covered with powdered sugar. Noteworthy is the variation filled with whipped cream or "crema pasticcera".

Schiacciata con l'uva – Sweetened bread dough with black grapes of the Tuscan classic "Canaiolo" type, sprinkled with sugar and rosemary, typical of harvest time (try that of the *La sosta de' golosi*, Via di Orsanmichele, no. 8/r).

Tiramisù – The most classic of Tuscan sweets containing coffee, ladyfingers and mascarpone. The region contends its paternity with Veneto, where it seems to have been introduced under the name of "Zuppa del Duca". It was renamed due to the exciting properties it seems to acquire with the addition of coffee to the liqueur in which the ladyfingers are soaked. A delicious variation is the one combining two products typical of Tuscany: "Biscotti di Prato" instead of the ladyfingers, soaked in a mixture of Vin Santo and coffee.

Torta al cioccolato del Pistocchi – Tasting this sweet whose recipe has been jealously kept secret is a unique experience for chocolate-lovers. It is, in fact, a flat cake made only of cocoa through a particular procedure that makes it unmistakable and inimitable, with a fragrance and a flavor without equal the world over (*Pistocchi*, Via Ponte di Mezzo, no. 20).

Torta al semolino – A luscious combination of cream of wheat and melted chocolate resting on a crust of sweet pastry.

Torta della nonna – A delicious pie formed of two disks of sweet pastry filled with "crema pasticcera" and covered with pine nuts and powdered sugar *(see photo p. 216)*. There also exists a **torta del nonno,** which has a heart of cocoa cream and a surface covered with drops of chocolate.

Zuccotto – The historic dish served at the court of the Medici, made of sponge cake, ricotta, chocolate and cream dampened with Alkermes. With its dome shape, commemorative of that of Brunelleschi, it was usually served on Easter Day; now it can be found all year round.

Zuppa inglese – An ice-cream cake evolved from the primordial Sienese sweet called "Zuppa del Duca", rich in ingredients such as sponge cake soaked in Alkermes and rum, whipped cream and liquid cream. It was so fashionable in the colony of British intellectuals and merchants who settled in Florence in the 18th and 19th centuries that it was named for them.

Recipes

Starters, snacks, savory pies and luncheon dishes

Coccoli (Fried dough)

Utensils: deep pan, 1 breadboard, 1 bowl
Preparation time: 20 min. + 2 hr. rising time
Cooking time: 20 min.
Ingredients per 6 persons:
– 3 ¼ cups of flour
– 1 cube of brewer's yeast
– 2 ½ tablespoons of butter
– seed oil for frying and salt

Preparation:
① Dissolve the yeast in ½ cup of warm water.
② Pour the flour in a cone shape onto a breadboard or table and add the yeast and water mixture.
③ Add the softened butter and knead to obtain a smooth, malleable dough.
④ Place the dough in a bowl, set it aside to rest in a warm place for about 2 hr., covered with a cloth.
⑤ With floured hands, form balls of dough the size of a walnut.
⑥ Fry them a few at a time in sizzling hot oil until they are puffed and well browned.
⑦ Drain them on paper towels, salt and serve hot.

There also exists a variation of larger size to be filled with Tuscan charcuterie.

🍷 Chianti Classico, Chianti Rufina and Pomino Rosso

Pasta and soups

Crespelle alla fiorentina (Filled crêpes Florentine style)

Utensils: medium-sized bowl and casserole, wooden spoon, wire whisk, ladle, rounded-tip spatula, 12-13 in. round pan, oven-proof dish.
Preparation time: white sauce 5 min., 10 min. each crêpe + 1 hr. resting time, spinach 20 min.

Cooking time: white sauce 20 min., 2 min. each crêpe, 15 min. in a moderate oven (350°F)

Ingredients for batter for 4 persons:
– 2 eggs
– 1 cup of flour type 0
– 1 cup of milk
– ¼ cup of butter
– 1 pinch of salt

Preparation:
① Beat the eggs well, then add the flour and milk, the melted butter and the salt; stir well to form a smooth batter. Let rest in the refrigerator for 1 hr.
② Heat a little butter in the pan and pour a ladleful of batter into it, letting the batter spread over the whole surface. Turn the crêpe with the aid of a rounded-tip spatula.
③ Continue in this way until all of the dough is used, buttering the bottom of the pan each time.

Ingredients for the white sauce:
– ¼ cup of butter
– ½ cup of flour type 0
– 2 cups of milk
– 1 sprinkling of nutmeg
– salt

Preparation:
① Melt the butter in the casserole over hot water. Add the sifted flour all at once and stir rapidly with a wooden spoon to keep lumps from forming.
② Pour in the hot milk and continue stirring until the cream is smooth.
③ Remove from heat, salt and flavor with nutmeg.

Ingredients for the filling:
– ¾ cup of ricotta
– ½ lb. of spinach
– 1 egg
– grated parmigiano as desired
– nutmeg
– a few cherry tomatoes or tablespoons of tomato purée

Preparation:

① Boil the spinach; squeeze it to remove the excess liquid and blend it. Add the ricotta, the egg, a handful of parmigiano and a little nutmeg and stir the mixture well.

② Spread the filling on the crêpes and roll them like canneloni.

③ Place them in an ovenproof dish and cover them with the white sauce, the tomatoes and a little grated parmigiano.

④ Brown the top for 15 min. in a preheated oven.

⑤ Serve hot.

🍷 Colli dell'Etruria Centrale Novello, Chianti Novello

Pasta al sugo scappato o finto (Pasta with 'imitation sauce')

Utensils: large pan (preferably terracotta), deep pot, saucepan
Preparation time: 20 min.
Cooking time: 40 min.
Ingredients for 4 persons:
– 1 lb. of short pasta (fusilli, macaroni, conchiglie, etc.)
– 1 ¾ cups of canned tomatoes
– 3 large carrots
– 3 large red onions
– 3 stalks of celery
– 1 bunch of parsley
– 1 bunch of basil
– ½ cup of olive oil
– ½ cup of Chianti
– salt and hot red pepper
– pecorino
– fresh sage and rosemary (optional)

Preparation:

① Chop the vegetables and sauté them in the pan with the olive oil on low heat for about 20 min.

② 5 min. before removing from the heat, add the wine and let it evaporate.

③ Meanwhile, heat the tomatoes in the saucepan; as soon as they reach the boiling point, add them to the sautéed chopped vegetables.

④ Salt, pepper and continue to cook for another 10 min.

⑤ Bring the water for the pasta to the boil, cook the pasta "al dente" and drain it, then pour it into the pot with the sauce. Stir the pasta into the sauce for a few minutes to let it absorb the flavor.

⑥ Serve with a sprinkling of pecorino.

In a tasty variation, the sauce is blended to obtain a delicious cream that can be spread on hot toasted rounds of bread as an excellent appetizer.

🍷 Chianti

Risotto ai carciofi di Empoli (Risotto with Empoli artichokes)

Utensils: large pan
Preparation time: 20 min.
Cooking time: 25 min.
Ingredients per 4 persons:
– 1 ½ cups of rice, risotto type
– 4 large artichokes
– 2 cloves of garlic
– ¼ cup of butter
– 4 cups of stock (soup cube acceptable)
– grated pecorino (the "fossa senese" type is excellent)
– olive oil
– salt and black pepper
– fennel seed
– thyme

Preparation:

① In the large pan, lightly brown the garlic and thyme in a little olive oil and half of the butter. Add the artichokes, cleaned and sliced fine, then salt and brown, adding a ladleful of broth.

② Add the rice, stir and toast it over high heat for a few minutes, then gradually add the stock, one ladleful at a time, stirring constantly.

③ Remove from the heat; before serving, stir well with the remaining butter, the pecorino and the fennel seed.

④ Serve hot with a sprinkling of pepper.

This risotto is very good even without the artichokes, passing directly to the toasting of the rice. In this case the pecorino must absolutely be of the "fossa" type, well aged.

🍷 Sparkling Bianco Vergine Valdichiana

Tagliatelle di farina di castagna (Chestnut flour tagliatelle)

Utensils: breadboard, rolling pin (or pasta machine), deep pot
Preparation time: 20 min. + 30 min. resting time
Cooking time: 5 min.

Ingredients for 4 persons for the dough:
– 1 cup of chestnut flour
– 2 ½ cups of wheat flour
– 4 eggs
– 1 pinch of salt

Preparation of the pasta:
① Sift the two kinds of flour together onto the breadboard in the shape of a cone. Form a hole in the middle and break the eggs into it; add a pinch of salt and knead well to obtain a smooth, soft ball of dough.
② Set the dough aside to rest for 30 min, covered with a sheet of plastic, in a cool place but not refrigerated.
③ Roll the dough, not too thin, with the rolling pin (or pasta machine) and cut the tagliatelle to a width of about 1/3 in.
④ Sprinkle the breadboard with a little flour to keep the tagliatelle from sticking to it, and let them rest 5 min.
⑤ Bring to the boil abundant water, add a little rock salt and 1 tablespoon of olive oil to keep the pasta from sticking together as it cooks. Cook the tagliatelle for 5 min.

Ingredients for the sauce:
– 1 cup of fresh sheep's-milk ricotta
– ½ cup of hot milk
– 1 tablespoon of chopped walnuts
– 1 tablespoon of aromatic herbs (sage, oregano, rosemary, thyme) chopped fine
– 1 clove of garlic chopped fine
– 1 pinch of salt and pepper

Preparation of the sauce:
① Mix the ricotta, chopped fine, with all of the other ingredients.
② Drain the tagliatelle and mix them with this sauce; sprinkle with black pepper and parmigiano to taste.

🍷 Colli dell'Etruria Centrale Bianco, Rosato di Carmignano

Topini ('Little mice' – Potato gnocchi)

Utensils: deep pot, potato masher, breadboard
Preparation time: 30 min.
Cooking time: 30 min. + 5 min.
Ingredients for 6/8 persons:
– 1 ½ lb. of medium-sized red potatoes
– 1 ¾ cups of white flour
– 1 egg
– salt to taste
– 1 tablespoon of olive oil

Preparation:
① Put the potatoes in a pot filled with cold water, bring to the boil and cook them for 30 min. (or 15 min. after the whistle starts to blow in a pressure cooker). Peel the potatoes and mash them with the potato masher directly on the breadboard.
② Sift the flour onto the potatoes, add the egg and a pinch of salt. Knead rapidly with the hands to obtain a soft mixture that does not stick to the fingers; otherwise, add more flour.
③ Form the mixture into a ball, then cut from it pieces of dough, rolling them into cylinders about ⅓ in. thick.
④ Cut the cylinders into pieces ¾ in. wide and place them on floured trays.
⑤ Boil them a pot of salted water, adding some olive oil to keep the "topini" from sticking together while cooking.
⑥ As the "topini" rise to the surface, scoop them out with a sieve.
⑦ Dress them as preferred with simple tomato sauce, meat sauce, walnut sauce, or pesto, and sprinkle them with parmigiano.

🍷 Sant'Antimo Pinot Nero, Bianco dell'Empolese

Tortelli di patate mugellani (Tortelli with potato filling Mugello style)

Utensils: deep pot (or pressure cooker), another deep pot, potato masher, saucepan, small pan, breadboard, pasta cutter
Preparation time: 30 min. for the pasta
Cooking time: 5 min.
Ingredients for filling for 6 persons:
– 4 lb. of white potatoes
– 6 cloves of chopped garlic

– 4 tablespoons of grated parmigiano or pecorino
– 1 bunch of parsley
– 1 pinch of nutmeg (optional)
– salt, pepper to taste, olive oil

Preparation:

① Boil the potatoes in their skins in abundant salted water (with the pressure cooker, 15 min. after the whistle).

② Peel them while hot and mash them on the floured breadboard.

③ In the saucepan, sauté in olive oil for a few minutes the coarsely chopped garlic, chopped parsley and parmigiano, adding salt, pepper and nutmeg (optional).

④ Add the sautéed mixture to the potatoes and knead well to mix the ingredients.

Ingredients for pasta dough for 6 persons:
– 8 cups of flour type 00
– 6 eggs
– 5 tablespoons of olive oil, salt

Preparation:

① Sift the flour onto the breadboard in the form of a cone, add the whole eggs, the salt and enough water to form the dough. Knead until the dough is smooth and even, then roll the dough thin and cut it in strips about 3 in. wide and long.

② Place a tablespoonful of the filling at the center of each strip at a distance of around 1-1 ½ in. Fold over each strip of pasta, shaping the tortelli by pressing well with the hands, then cut them into squares with the pasta cutter. Continue until all of the dough of both kinds has been used.

③ Boil the tortelli a few minutes in abundant water; they are done when they rise to the surface.

④ Dress them as desired with porcini mushroom sauce, wild boar sauce, meat sauce or butter and fresh sage.

🍷 Pomino Rosso, Rosato di Carmignano

Meat, fish, and side dishes

Arista alla fiorentina (Pork roast Florentine style)

Utensils: butcher's twine, oven pan

Preparation time: 15 min.
Cooking time: 2 hr. in a moderate oven (350ºF)
Ingredients for 6 persons:
– 3 ½ lb. of loin of pork, preferably with the bone
– 3 cloves of garlic and fennel seed (optional)
– 3 twigs of fresh rosemary, olive oil, salt and pepper

Preparation:
① Chop the herbs with 2 tablespoons of salt and pepper; score the meat with a sharp knife and fill the slits with this mixture, which flavors it intensely and makes it easier to remove from the bone.
② Bind the roast with the twine; place it in the pan and sprinkle it with olive oil.
③ Roast in the oven, basting frequently with the meat juices. When it is almost done, raise the heat to 390°F to brown it.
④ Using a sharp knife, remove the bone.
⑤ Serve the roast with its juices, either hot or lukewarm.

The ideal accompaniment consists of potatoes cut in cubes added to the roasting pan 30 min. before the roast is done.

🍷 Chianti Novello, Chianti Classico dei Colli Fiorentini

Baccalà alla fiorentina (Salt cod Florentine style)

Utensils: large pan
Preparation time: 20 min.
Cooking time: 30 min.
Ingredients for 6 persons:
– 2 lb. of salt cod already soaked and boned
– 1 ½ cups of tomato sauce or 2 tablespoons of tomato paste diluted in a cup of water
– 2 or 3 cloves of garlic
– a bunch of parsley
– flour as required
– olive oil, black pepper and hot red pepper to taste
– 6 slices of Tuscan bread

Preparation:
① Heat the olive oil with 2 cloves of garlic in the pan, cut the salt cod into medium-sized pieces and dust them with flour.
② Remove the garlic when golden brown and add the salt cod to the pan, browning it well on both sides.

③ Add a pinch of black pepper, of red pepper and the tomato sauce and cook for another 15-20 min.

④ Sprinkle with chopped parsley and serve on slices of toasted Tuscan bread rubbed with garlic.

🍷 Rosato di Carmignano, Pomino Bianco

Carabaccia (Onion soup)

Utensils: terracotta pot, 6 soup dishes
Preparation time: 90 min.
Cooking time: 1 hr.
Ingredients for 6 persons:
– 2 lb. of red onions
– 2 medium-sized carrots
– 1 stalk of white celery
– 2 cups of vegetable stock
– 6 tablespoons of olive oil, salt and pepper to taste
– 6 slices of toasted Tuscan bread
– 6 poached eggs (optional)
– 1 ½ cups of peas, broad beans or chickpeas (optional)

Preparation:
① Chop the vegetables and put them in the pot with the olive oil, salt and pepper; cover and cook over very low heat for about 30 min.
② Add the stock and continue cooking for 30 min.
③ Toast the bread and place a slice in each soup dish; pour the soup over the toasted bread and sprinkle with parmigiano and pepper.
④ Serve hot; let rest a few minutes before bringing to the table.

The richer version calls for fresh boiled legumes to be added when the soup is nearly done, and a poached egg added to each portion just before serving. If instead 2 sausages and 2 oz. of streaky bacon or Colonnata lard are browned in the pot before adding the onions, the resulting soup is called "Cipollata", another tasty recipe. The recipe for "Carabaccia" is a medieval one that has come down to us, although the original called for almonds soaked in vinegar with a little sugar and cinnamon, in a sweet-and-sour version. The origin of the name is rather uncertain since one version resembles the Greek term for 'boat in the shape of a nutshell', which vaguely suggests a soup tureen, while another derives instead from Spanish cooking.

🍷 Pomino Bianco, Rosato di Carmignano

Fritto misto alla fiorentina (Mixed fried meats and vegetables)

Utensils: large frying pan
Preparation time: 20 min.
Cooking time: 15 for the meat, 5-7 min. for the vegetables
Ingredients for 4 persons:
– 1 chicken cut in pieces (about 2 lbs.)
– ½ rabbit (about 1 lb.)
– 8 lamb cutlets
– fresh, tender vegetables (zucchini flowers, carrots, artichokes, potatoes, boiled cauliflower) quantities as desired
– 4 eggs
– flour and breadcrumbs as required
– oil for frying, salt

Preparation:
① Clean and dry the chicken and rabbit, then cut them in pieces and dredge them in flour. Dry the lamb cutlets, dredge them in flour, dip them in beaten egg and coat them with breadcrumbs.
② Clean the vegetables and divide them into small parts (cut the zucchini and carrots à julienne, the artichokes and potatoes in wedges; divide the cauliflower, boiled but still firm, into flowerets) leaving the zucchini flowers whole; coat the vegetables with flour.
③ Beat the eggs with a pinch of salt; dip first the meat, then the vegetables into the beaten eggs.
④ Meanwhile heat the oil in the frying pan. When it is hot but not boiling, fry the pieces of meat over moderate heat, raising the heat when they are nearly done to brown them. Drain them and place them on paper towels in a dish.
⑤ Fry the vegetables, a few at a time, for a few minutes. Drain them and add them to the dish with the meat; add salt.
⑥ Serve at once with slices of lemon.

Originally, as is still the custom by some trattorie in the country, the mixed fry also included lamb brains and sweetbreads.

🍷 Colli dell'Etruria Centrale Novello, sweet sparkling Bianco Vergine Valdichiana

Lesso rifatto o francesina (Twice cooked meat)

Utensils: large deep pot
Preparation time: 20 min.

Cooking time: 20 min.
Ingredients for 6 persons:
– 1 lb. of boiled beef, boned, cut in medium-sized pieces
– 2 lb. of onions
– 1 lb. of tomatoes, seeded and skinned (or 3 tablespoons of tomato paste diluted in a cup of hot water)
– 2 cloves of garlic
– fresh sage and bay leaf
– olive oil
– salt and pepper
– 6 slices of toasted Tuscan bread

Preparation:
① Brown the chopped garlic, sage and bay leaf in olive oil.
② Coarsely chop the onions and add them to the pot with the herbs. Cover and cook until softened over low heat, stirring frequently (add a little water if necessary) for about 15 min.
③ Add the boiled beef and simmer covered for 10 min., stirring frequently to let it absorb the flavors.
④ Add the tomatoes and cook covered, adding salt and pepper to taste (add a little water if necessary).
⑤ Simmer for another 10 min. Remove the cover and reduce the sauce if necessary, raising the heat.
⑥ Serve hot with slices of bread.

Some cooks like to give this recipe additional flavor by adding to the sauté 2 oz. of streaky bacon and ½ glass of wine immediately after having added the meat. Another version calls for cubed potatoes instead of onions.

🍷 Pomino Rosso, Chianti di Montespertoli

Ossibuchi alla fiorentina (Shin steak Florentine style)

Utensils: 2 large, deep pans
Preparation time: 20 min.
Cooking time: 2 hr. and 30 min.
Ingredients for 4 persons:
– 4 veal shin steaks, about ½ lb. each
– 2 carrots
– 2 small onions
– 1 clove of garlic
– 1 stalk of celery

– 1 ½ cups of canned tomatoes or 4 tablespoons of tomato paste
– flour as required
– thyme
– 1 ½ cups of white wine (preferably dry Vin Santo)
– 4 tablespoons of olive oil
– salt and pepper

Preparation:
① Sauté in olive oil the finely chopped celery, carrots, onions, thyme and garlic.
② Add the tomatoes (when using tomato paste, dilute it in abundant water), salt and pepper, then bring to the boil.
③ Make small cuts around the edges of the shin steaks to keep the meat from curling as it cooks. Dust them with flour and brown them well in a little olive oil in the other pan. Add the wine, the pepper, and let evaporate.
④ Pour over the meat the tomato sauce prepared in the other pan and cook over low heat for about 2 hr., turning the meat occasionally, until the sauce thickens; the shin steaks should remain tender.
⑤ Serve hot accompanied by fresh peas or spinach cooked and reheated in melted butter.

🍷 Vernaccia di San Gimignano, Colli dell'Etruria Centrale Rosato

Peposo alla fornacina (Peppery meat stew)

Utensils: wide deep pan
Preparation time: 10 min.
Cooking time: 3 hr.
Ingredients for 4 persons:
– 2 lbs. of beef (stew meat)
– 1 ½ cups of peeled, pureed tomatoes
– 4 cloves of garlic
– 2-4 teaspoons of ground black pepper
– 1 glass of Chianti
– salt
– water as required

Preparation:
① Place in the pan the cubed meat, the peeled garlic, the tomatoes and the salt and pepper; add cold water to cover.
② Cook over low heat for about 2 hr.

③ Add the wine, adjust the salt and cook for about one more hour.
④ Serve hot.

A simple dish, but exceptionally tasty thanks to its long cooking time.

🍷 Carmignano Riserva, Morellino di Scansano

Trippa alla fiorentina (Tripe Florentine style)

Utensils: large pan
Preparation time: 30 min.
Cooking time: 1 hr.
Ingredients for 4 persons:
– 2 lb. of tripe already washed, cleaned and boiled
– 1 onion
– 1 carrot
– 3 stalks of celery
– 1 glass of Chianti
– mixed aromatic herbs (mint, laurel, rosemary, sage, etc.)
– 1 ¼ cups of puréed tomatoes (or 3 tablespoons of tomato paste diluted in 1 cup of water)
– 6 tablespoons of olive oil, salt and black pepper
– 6 tablespoons of grated parmigiano

Preparation:

① Sauté the finely chopped vegetables with the herbs in olive oil for a few minutes. Add the tripe cut into strips; stew gently, stirring often to keep it from sticking to the pan.

② Add the wine and let it evaporate, add the tomato, salt and pepper and cook covered over low heat until the sauce thickens.

③ Remove from the heat, add 3 tablespoons of parmigiano, mixing well, and let rest for 5 min.

④ Serve in individual plates with a sprinkling of pepper and more parmigiano.

Some cooks prefer to omit the wine and to sauté the tripe a little longer before adding the tomatoes. Others add potatoes along with the tomatoes, to make the dish even heartier.

🍷 Colli dell'Etruria Centrale Novello, Chianti Classico

Cakes, pies and cookies

Cenci (Fried cookies)

Utensils: breadboard, rolling pin (or pasta machine), pasta cutter with zigzag edges, deep frying pan
Preparation time: 30 min.
Cooking time: 3-4 min.
Ingredients for 6/8 persons:
– 2 ½ cups of flour type 00
– 1 cup of sugar
– 4 eggs
– 1 teaspoon of vanilla-flavored baking powder
– 1 packet of vanilla flavoring
– 1 grated lemon rind
– 1 glass of white wine
– oil or lard for frying
– powdered sugar to garnish

Preparation:

① Sift the flour onto the breadboard and add the sugar, eggs, lemon rind, baking powder, vanilla flavoring and wine.

② Knead to form a firm, smooth dough, then roll it rather thin.

③ Cut the dough into diamond shapes or strips with the pasta cutter, pressing the strips in the middle to give them the shape of a bow.

④ Heat the oil or lard and fry the strips of pasta a few at a time on both sides for a few minutes.

⑤ Serve while still hot, sprinkled with powdered sugar and with a glass of aged Vin Santo.

🍷 Sparkling Bianco di Pitigliano, Pomino Vin Santo Bianco Amabile

Pan di ramerino (Rosemary bread)

Utensils: breadboard, pan, oven tray
Preparation time: 20 min. + 2 hr. rising time
Cooking time: 30 min. in a moderate oven (350°F)
Ingredients per 4-5 small loaves:
– 4 cups of flour type 0
– 1 oz. of brewer's yeast, 2 ½ tablespoons of sugar
– 2 cups of sultana raisins
– 2 twigs of fresh rosemary
– 4 tablespoons of olive oil, a pinch of salt

Preparation:

① Sift the flour onto the breadboard, form a hole in the center and pour into it the sugar and the yeast previously dissolved in a little warm water. Knead to form a firm, compact dough; flour the ball of dough, cover it with a kitchen towel and leave it to rise for about 1 hr. in a dry place.

② Meanwhile, warm the olive oil with a sprig of fresh rosemary and the unsoaked raisins. Remove from the heat and let cool.

③ Knead the dough again, add the olive oil, raisins, crumbled rosemary and salt; continue to knead well.

④ Divide the dough into 4-5 small loaves. Place them well separated on the floured oven tray and let them rise again for another 45 min.

⑤ Score the surface with a cross, brush with olive oil and bake. Serve hot or cold as preferred.

These leaves are traditionally eaten at Easter time, on Holy Thursday, as re-evocation of the Last Supper, and are blessed by the priests in the churches.

🍷 Vin Santo del Chianti Classico

Schiacciata alla fiorentina (Traditional Florentine cake)

Utensils: wire whisk, bowl, rectangular oven pan 12 × 10 in.
Preparation time: 20 min.
Cooking time: 35-40 min. in a moderate oven (350°F)
Ingredients for 6 persons:
– 2 whole eggs
– 6 tablespoons of olive oil
– 6 tablespoons of sugar
– 12 tablespoons of flour type 00
– 12 tablespoons of milk
– 1 grated orange rind
– juice of 1 orange
– 1 packet of baking powder, 1 pinch of salt
– butter to butter the pan, powdered sugar

Preparation:
① Place in the bowl 2 eggs, 6 tablespoons of olive oil, 6 tablespoons of sugar, 12 tablespoons of flour and 10 tablespoons of milk; stir well with the slotted spoon.
② Add the grated orange rind, its juice and the pinch of salt, stirring well to obtain a smooth, even dough. If it is too thick, add another 2 tablespoons of milk. Then add the baking power and mix well.
③ Butter and flour the pan, pour the dough into it and bake in a preheated oven 35-40 min.
④ For the first 5 min., bake only from below, then continue baking with heat from both above and below.
⑤ Remove the cake from the oven and let it cool. Sprinkle with powdered sugar.

This simple sweet baked for Carnival can be filled with "crema pasticcera", Nutella® or whipped cream. It is frequently decorated on top with a lily, symbol of the city of Florence.

🍷 Elba Ansonica Passito, Moscadello di Montalcino Vendemmia Tardiva

Schiacciata con l'uva (Cake with grapes)

Utensils: bowl, breadboard, deep rectangular pan
Preparation time: 30 min. + 1 hr. and 40 min. rising time
Cooking time: 30 min. in a moderate oven (350°F)

Ingredients for 6 persons:
– 3 cups of flour
– ¾ oz. of brewer's yeast
– 2 lbs. of small black wine grapes (preferably seeded)
– 8 tablespoons of sugar
– 4 tablespoons of olive oil
– 1 glass of red wine (Morellino Scansano, Chianti)
– 1 sprig of rosemary or 1 teaspoon of fennel seed (optional)

Preparation:
① Dissolve the yeast in a little warm water and add it to the sifted flour in the bowl along with 4 tablespoons of olive oil.
② Knead the dough and let it rest for 1 hr. covered by a cloth in a warm place.
③ Oil the baking pan and spread half of the dough in it.
④ Add ⅔ of the grapes, washed and dried, to the dough, pressing them into it. Sprinkle over it 3 tablespoons of sugar.
⑤ Cover with the remaining dough, pressing it against the edges of the pan. Add the rest of the grapes and sugar.
⑥ Dribble the surface with olive oil and set aside to rise 40 min.
⑦ Before baking, dampen with a glass of red wine. Sprinkle with a few needles of fresh rosemary or fennel seed (optional).
⑧ Bake in a preheated oven for about 30 min. until the upper crust is lightly browned.

The choice of grapes for this cake is fundamental. The best are the typically Tuscan Canaiolo grapes.

🍷 Vin Santo del Chianti Classico

Torta al semolino (Cream of wheat cake)

Utensils: a double boiler or 2 saucepans, one of them smaller in size, a deep pan, 10 in. round cake pan, brush for sweets
Preparation time: 20 min. +1 hr. of resting time
Cooking time: 5 min. +15 min. in a moderate oven
Ingredients for 6 persons:
– 1 cup of semolina
– 1 packet of vanilla flavoring
– 1 ¼ cups of sugar
– 2 cups of milk
– 1 stick of vanilla

– 7 oz. of unsweetened chocolate
– 1 lemon rind
– readymade pie dough (see the following recipe for preparation), powdered sugar to garnish

Preparation:

① Pour the milk into the saucepan with the sugar, vanilla flavoring, lemon rind and the stick of vanilla cut half-through lengthwise. As soon as it comes to the boil, remove the vanilla and add the semolina. Cook over moderate heat for about 7 min., stirring occasionally to keep it from sticking.

② Remove the semolina from the heat and let it cool.

③ Spread the pie dough in the buttered cake pan; prick it with a fork and bake it for a few minutes in a hot oven.

④ Pour the semolina mixture into the cake pan, leveling the surface, and bake it for 15 min.

⑤ In the meantime, melt the unsweetened chocolate over hot water.

⑥ Remove the cake from the oven, let it cool for 5 min., then spread it evenly with the chocolate.

⑦ Refrigerate for 1 hr. and serve sprinkled with powdered sugar.

🍷 Vin Santo dell'Empolese, Colli dell'Etruria Centrale Vin Santo

Torta della nonna (Grandmother's pie)

Utensils: bowl, strainer, deep 10-12 in. round cake pan
Preparation time: 45 min. + 30 min. resting time for the pie dough
Cooking time: 20 min. for the cream + 40 min. for the cake in a moderate oven
Ingredients for 6-8 persons:
– 2 ½ cups of flour
– ⅔ cup of butter
– ¾ cup of sugar
– 1 whole egg, 1 yolk
– ½ packet of vanilla-flavored baking powder
– a pinch of salt
– 1 handful of pine nuts and blanched almonds
– grated rind of an organically grown lemon
– vanilla flavored powdered sugar

For the cream:
– 2 cups of whole fresh milk

– grated rind of an organically grown lemon
– ½ cup of sugar, 2 egg yolks
– ½ cup of flour type 00
– half a teaspoon of potato starch

Preparation of the cream:

① Set aside one-fourth of the milk and add to it the sugar with the grated lemon rind.

② Add to the remaining milk the egg yolks, the flour and potato starch and mix in the blender.

③ Pour the mixture through a strainer into the milk with the sugar and lemon.

④ Pour this cream into a large pot and cook over low heat for about 20 min., stirring constantly to keep it from sticking.

⑤ When the cream thickens, remove it from the heat and let it cool (it can also be placed in the refrigerator).

Preparation of the sweet pie dough:

① Melt the butter in a saucepan taking care that it does not burn; let it cool.

② Mix well in a bowl or on a breadboard the sugar, the sifted baking powder, the whole egg and the yolk, then the sifted flour, the salt and lastly the butter, melted and slightly cooled, and the lemon rind.

③ Knead the mixture vigorously to form a smooth, even dough. Shape it into a ball, divide it in two and refrigerate for about 30 min.

④ Spread a round of pie dough about ⅓ in. thick over the bottom and edges of the buttered cake pan lined with oven paper. Prick the dough with a fork; pour the cooled cream into it, leveling the surface.

⑤ Spread the second round of pie dough, about ⅓ in. thick, on a sheet of floured oven paper, so that it will be easier to pick it up and place on top of the pie.

⑥ Press the edges of the dough together to seal the pie, sprinkle the surface with pine nuts and broken almonds and bake in a preheated oven.

⑦ Remove from the oven, sprinkle with powdered sugar and serve while still warm.

This pie has no precise date of origin, but wherever you go you will find it, served simple or frequently accompanied by a fruit sauce or hot Nutella®. There also exists a version called Torta del Nonno, or Grandfather's pie, to which 2 oz. of unsweetened chocolate melted over hot water are added and mixed slowly and thoroughly. When the pie has been removed from the oven and allowed to cool, it is sprinkled with unsweetened cocoa. To shorten the preparation time you can use readymade frozen pie dough; remember to take it out of the freezer and leave it at room temperature for at least an hour before using.

🍷 Sant'Antimo Vin Santo, Elba Ansonica Passito, Moscadello di Montalcino

Zuccotto (Ricotta pudding)

Utensils: dome-shaped mold, 2 bowls, brush for sweets
Preparation time: 1 hr. + 5 hr. refrigeration time
Ingredients for 6 persons:
– ½ lb. of readymade sponge cake
– 2 cups of whipped cream
– 1 cup of sheep's-milk ricotta
– 3 oz. of flaked unsweetened chocolate
– 2 ½ oz. of unsweetened cocoa
– 10 almonds, ¼ cup of candied fruit
– 2 tablespoons of powdered sugar
– Alkermes to dampen and 1 small glass of sweet liqueur

Preparation:
① Cut the sponge cake in rectangular pieces, place them in a semispherical pudding mould, then sprinkle lightly with a mixture of Alkermes and sweet liqueur, leaving some of the pieces dry to be used for the last layer.
② In a bowl, sift together the unsweetened cocoa and the powdered sugar, then add half of the whipped cream and the ricotta.
③ Add the chocolate, the chopped almonds and the candied fruit to the other half of the whipped cream.
④ Fill the mold with a layer of cream, chocolate, almonds and candied fruit. Lightly beat the mold against the table to make the mixture settle well, then add the other filling of cream, ricotta and cocoa.
⑤ Cover with the remaining pieces of sponge cake, press well and brush with the remaining juice. Refrigerate for at least 4 hr.
⑥ Turn out the mold onto a large plate and serve.

🍷 Pomino Vin Santo Rosso Secco

GROSSETO AT THE TABLE

Grosseto, the southernmost city in Tuscany, has a territory that stretches on one side from the sea to the promontory of Argentario with the islands of Giglio and Giannutri; on the other, as far as Monte Amiata in the eastern part, which includes the heart of that vast area called Maremma. Although its position might suggest development along the coastline, this is not the case. On the contrary, the sea has been its limitation for centuries. The real development of the city took place only recently, during the years between the two world wars, when the great project of draining the marshes that obstructed passage toward the sea was definitively concluded.

The history of this territory boasts Etruscan origins. The numerous necropolises that have come to light show that the area at that time underwent notable expansion both agricultural (the Etruscans were the first to drain some of the marshes in the territory) and commercial; but the harsh nature of the land led the ancient civilization to push inland toward more hospitable zones, bordering on the mountains. This expansion led to the founding of smaller villages that however became important centers of defense for the territory, especially in medieval times. The area was repeatedly struck by epidemics and famines which kept it sparsely populated at least up to the 16th century when, thanks to the Medici family, the real work of draining the marshes began, bringing new inhabitants to settle on long-abandoned land. Here we find in fact 'jewel' villages clinging to steep hillsides or built on walls of tufa stone whose ancient structures can still be seen today, such as Castiglione della Pescaia, Massa Marittima, Pitigliano, Sorano and Sovana.

The environmental improvement has recently led to the amplification of tourist resources and the reassessment of both naturalist elements – such as the splendid Uccellina Park, and the area around the thermal baths of Saturnia – and the fine food of the territory. The cooking of Grosseto is closely linked to its inland area and to the wild plains and hills of Maremma. Contrary to what might be thought, considering the close proximity of the sea, this area was also influenced by its submission to the city of Siena, with which it shares some dishes with only a few variations. Then as now, its cuisine is based on simple, inexpensive ingredients, those most commonly found every day such as vegetables, wild herbs, mushrooms and the many cereals used to make bread, as well as the products of cattle-breeding (the figure of the "buttero", the Maremma cowboy astride his horse, is famous) and sheep-farming. Exceptionally good are the fresh cheeses – such as ricotta, which is also found smoked, and which is used around Easter to prepare **schiaccia** – and the aged ones, like the many kinds of pecorino, excellent when accompanied by wine jelly made from the famous labels of the area. The different kinds of meat are also excellent, and are used in many dishes such as lamb **buglione,** a very special stew whose recipe may have been inherited from the Jewish community; without forgetting the pork raised here, whose various kinds of charcuterie include **salsiccia con le patate**, a succulent variation of the sausage and potatoes dish typical of Monte Amiata.

Among the innumerable soups, one above all can be deemed the symbol of Maremma. Called **acquacotta** (literally, cooked water), it was in the past the daily fare of cowboys, made with the poorest of ingredients such as vegetables, bread, pecorino and eggs. And then there is **zuppa lombarda**, with beans and bread rubbed with garlic. Among the first courses can still be found the pasta dish served on great occasions: **maccheroni maremmani**, consisting of pappardelle dressed with a sauce made of chicken and rabbit livers and interior organs, sausage, walnuts, mushrooms and tomatoes, which is not just a first course but a meal in itself. Grosseto contends with Siena the creation of the famous **pici**, a kind of thick spaghetti made of water and flour alone, which is the perfect accompaniment to many sauces, of both meat and mushrooms, and **gnudi**, a sort of 'naked' ravioli, that is, the filling alone without its envelope of pasta. Among the sweets we also find a Grosseto version of the more famous Sienese **pan co' Santi**, made of walnuts, raisins and spices. And if you visit the Island of Giglio, you must try the rich, fragrant **panficato** containing dried figs, fruit preserved in liqueur and dried, cocoa and chocolate. Reigning supreme in the Grosseto area are wild boar, hare, and game in general, the essential elements of many first and second courses, such as pappardelle, roasts and stews, and excellent charcuterie such as sausages, salami and wild boar prosciutto.

Closer to the sea, in the lagoon of Orbetello, a fish-farming industry is now developing with the production of such species as the gilthead and sea bass. Eels are also grown there, used to prepare a very tasty Christmas soup; while salt cod is the main ingredient of what is known as **Paradiso di Pitigliano**. In Pitigliano, the influence of the Jewish community that lived there for centuries has been strong, so much so that the town has been called 'the little Jerusalem'. Today the few persons left from this group produce their typical kosher oil and wine. Renowned sweets closely linked to the history of the Jews in this area are **sfratto**, made with walnuts and honey and **bollo**, sweet bread flavored with anise. But the town is also known for its ovens and, even today, it is not unusual to catch an enticing whiff of fragrant newly baked bread in the air.

Among the various kinds of bread, sweet and savory, typical of the zone are **focaccia bastarda**, in the curious shape of a mushroom, made of flour, ricotta and Vin Santo and baked in "testi" at Easter time. The **focaccia di Pasqua salata** is instead a flat loaf made of ricotta, flour and spices. Another delicacy to be sampled is the **migliaccia di Pitigliano**, a sort of aromatic pancake to be eaten either alone or filled with ricotta. A great variety of cookies and ring-shaped sweets are prepared in the territory, and many of them contain aniseed, such as **ciaramito**. Among the many village fairs is one dedicated to the Roccalbenga cookie, held on the holiday of Ferragosto, where you can taste among other things the **biscotti di mezz'agosto** (mid-August cookies) made with aniseed and sweet wine, those **della Sposa** (of the bride), also containing aniseed and white wine, but savory rather than salty; not to mention the **brecciotto** made with olive oil, wine, sugar and flour. There are, in fact, cookies and biscuits for all tastes. A typical Easter sweet in the Orbetello area is the **scarsella orbetellana**, a ring-shaped cake flavored with anise and orange rind. Here, as in the rest of the region, excellent wines are produced. This zone is, in fact, the reign of the some of the world's most famous labels, such as **Morellino di Scansano** and then the excellent **Bianco di Pitigliano**, as well as **Montecucco**, **Monteregio di Massa Marittima**, **Capalbio**, **Ansonica dell'Argentario**, **Sovana** and **Parrina**, produced according to stringent rules that allow no adulteration. To be sampled are the different kinds of jelly made of wine, which are excellent as accompaniment to cheeses and grilled meat. Noteworthy among them are the one made of Bianco di Pitigliano, with its bitter-sweet tang, and the one made of Morellino di Scansano, sweeter and flavored with spices (we recommend those of the wine cellar *Ghiottornia*, at Via Roma, no. 111, Pitigliano).

GLOSSARY

Pasta and soups

Acquacotta – The 'poor' soup par excellence, destined in the past to the natives of the area, made of meat stock, bread and vegetables: onions, tomatoes, celery, carrots and fresh basil with the addition of toasted bread, olive oil, pecorino and eggs. Over the course of time the recipe has changed, being enriched with other ingredients, among them the eggs. Every year in August a fair dedicated to this dish is held at S. Fiora, on the slopes of Monte Amiata.

Caldaro – A tasty fish soup made with the catch of the day (both fish with bones and fish without) to which are added tomatoes, red hot pepper, stale bread, various herbs and frequently potatoes as well. It is a dish that is prepared with few variations along the entire Tyrrhenian coast.

Gnudi – Ravioli without their envelope of pasta, from which comes their name 'naked', made only of spinach, ricotta and pecorino. Rounded in shape, they have a very particular taste, ideal with meat sauce or simply with melted butter and fresh sage.

Maccheroni maremmani – "Pappardelle" with an especially rich, savory sauce, according to the ancient recipe that calls for chicken and rabbit livers and interior organs, sausage, bacon, walnuts, mushrooms and tomatoes.

Minestra della sciorna – A very special soup made of pureed beans, lard, vegetables and herbs. It is said to have been invented by gossipy housewives who, having wasted a lot of time, could not prepare a decent pasta, but had to put on the fire this soup with a shapeless, improvised pasta called "braciolelli" made directly over the pot by rubbing with the hands a mixture of flour and eggs. This may explain the origin of the name "sciorna", which means a silly woman who wastes her time chatting.

Pagnone – A simple soup made of stale bread and cauliflower.

Pappardelle al cinghiale – A dish whose origin is contended with other Tuscan provinces. At any rate, it will not be hard to find in the menus of numerous restaurants in the territory.

Pici con il sugo di cinghiale o di funghi porcini o di salsiccia – This pasta dish was one of the humble treats of the farmers who lived in this area who, not always having eggs available, made this kind of thick, long spaghetti. Today eggs can also be added to the dough, and the best dressing for the pici is a sauce of wild boar or porcini mushrooms, or even sausage. In August a fair is dedicated to it in Seggiano.

Tortello maremmano con spinaci – Pasta in the shape of a square, filled with spinach and ricotta, dressed with meat sauce and sprinkled with abundant pecorino. Throughout the territory of the province, many summer fairs dedicated to this dish are held; memorable among them are those of Roselle, Vetulonia and Monterotondo Marittimo.

Zuppa lombarda – A dish consisting of beans, bread rubbed with garlic and pepper. This 18th-century recipe was created at the time when workers from Lombardy came to this area for the land reclamation project.

Meat, fish, and side dishes

Buglione – A lamb stew in which the meat is marinated in wine, vinegar, carrots, onions and aromatic herbs (sage, rosemary and basil). The meat is browned with garlic, hot red pepper, and red wine and then cooked in stock and tomato sauce. It is served on slices of toasted bread. The town of Semproniano holds a fair for it in August. The origin of this recipe is lost in the remote past. It is also made mixed with other kinds of meat, and in this version it becomes very similar to the *Scottiglia* of Arezzo.

Cipolle alla grossetana – A savory side dish that also makes an excellent main dish, since the onions are scooped out and filled with a mixture of chopped onion, ground meat, sausage and herbs. They are then cooked in stock and white wine.

Lepre alla maremmana – A main dish consisting of hare marinated and brazed in red wine, to be accompanied by polenta. Due to the very particular nature of the dish and the requisite of extra-fresh meat, it is found only locally.

Paradiso di Pitigliano – A tasty main dish consisting of salt cod cooked without tomatoes, dressed with olive oil, parsley and pepper, and served on slices of toasted bread rubbed with garlic.

Scaveccio – A dish of very particular flavor made of eel, first fried and then marinated in vinegar, rosemary, sage, hot red pepper and garlic. It is sometimes made with small fry instead of eel.

Cakes, pies, cookies and liqueurs

Biscotti di mezz'agosto – Delicious, fragrant cookies in the shape of doughnuts about 12 in. in diameter, made of flour, yeast, anise and sweet vine. They are called 'mid-August cookies', because they were the snack eaten by farm workers during the summer threshing. In the town of Roccalbenga a fair is dedicated to them at "Ferragosto".

Biscotto con l'unto – Crunchy cookies in the form of doughnuts made with lard, sugar, flour, eggs, lemons and mint-flavored rosolio. The typical breakfast of the vineyard workers, they should be tasted with young wines.

Bollo – A sweet, rounded, very soft bread, flavored with aniseed, a legacy of Jewish cooking.

Brecciotto – Typical of the Roccalbenga area and made with olive oil, wine, aniseed, sugar and flour, its name derives from the nearby stone quarry. It is usually eaten as a dessert, accompanied by heavy, sweet wines.

Ciaccia di Pasqua – Typical of Easter, it is a loaf of leavened bread with the addition of eggs and pepper. When done, it is greased still further with melted lard. It is served on Easter Day at the beginning of the traditional meal.

Ciaccino – A sweet linked to the tradition of All Saints' Day, it is a flat loaf made with the traditional Tuscan bread dough, enriched with salt, pepper, olive oil, raisins and walnuts; excellent at breakfast or as a snack.

Ciaffagnoni – This is a crêpe whose origins date back to the 15th century, made of eggs and flour, to be eaten hot either in the sweet version spread with Nutella® or jam, or merely dusted with sugar; or in the salty version, with charcuterie and cheeses.

Ciaramito – A flat heart-shaped cake with a hole in the middle, typical of country tradition, made with eggs, flour, sugar, lard and aniseed.

Pan de' Santi – A soft, flat loaf containing walnuts, raisins, pepper and spices, typical of the feast of All Saints.

Scarsella Orbetellana – A ring-shaped cake made of flour, eggs, sugar, anise and orange rind, firm and crunchy in consistency, prepared for the Easter period and enriched in the center with a whole egg left in its shell. The origin of this sweet very probably dates from the time in which Spanish troops were stationed here, when it was given to child beggars.

Sfratto – A Christmas cake of elongated shape with a crunchy crust, filled with a mixture of walnuts, honey spices and orange rind. Among the many different explanations of its name, linked to the history of the Jewish people, is the one that says it originated in the 17th century in memory of the "sfratto" (eviction notice) presented to the Jews by the messenger of Grand Duke Cosimo II de' Medici. This messenger, in fact, knocked with a stick at the doors of families ordered to move into the ghetto at Pitigliano.

Taglioli di Castell'Azzara – Diamond-shaped cookies of very spicy taste, insofar as they contain pepper in addition to walnuts and honey. They were consumed by miners in the zone, along with a glass of wine.

Topi di Castell'Azzara – Tasty cookies in the shape of a half-moon made of pie dough with a rich, flavorful filling of walnuts, honey, spices and orange rind.

Tortello dolce di Pitigliano (*see photo*) – A square cake made of dough containing white wine with a filling of ricotta and sugar flavored with cinnamon, sprinkled when done with Alkermes and powdered sugar. It can be found either baked or fried.

Zuccherino di Maremma – Cookies in the shape of doughnuts made of eggs, sugar and flour and flavored with lemon, dusted with powdered sugar. Invented at the time of Italy's Unification as a teatime treat for the upper class ladies of the time, they are excellent also as dessert, accompanied by sweet Vin Santo.

Recipes

Pasta and soups

Acquacotta ('Cooked water' soup)

Utensils: large deep pot
Preparation time: 20 min.
Cooking time: 35-40 min.
Ingredients for 6/8 persons:
– 2 red onions
– 2 cloves of garlic
– 2 carrots
– 2 stalks of celery
– a few ripe tomatoes
– 4 cups of water
– 6 eggs
– 6 slices of Tuscan bread
– grated parmigiano or pecorino
– 1 hot red pepper
– olive oil
– salt

Preparation:
① Clean all of the vegetables and chop them coarsely.
② In the pan, sauté over high heat the onion, garlic and hot red pepper; lower the heat and cook slowly until the onions are done.
③ Add the other vegetables, salt, and stir gently to mix the flavors. Add water and simmer for about 20 min.
④ Gently break the eggs into the soup, leaving them whole, and poach them over low heat.
⑤ Place the slices of toasted bread in soup dishes, sprinkle them with abundant grated parmigiano or pecorino, and then pour the soup over them.
⑥ Serve hot.

A tasty version is the one that also calls for the addition of mushrooms of various kinds, to be sautéed with the vegetables.

🍷 Monteregio di Massa Marittima Rosato, Parrina Bianco

Pici con la briciolata (Pasta with crumble topping)

Utensils: breadboard, rolling pin, deep pot, saucepan
Preparation time: 30 min. + 30 min. resting time for the pasta dough
Cooking time: 5 min.
Ingredients for 8 persons:
– 6 ½ cups of flour
– lukewarm water as required
– 1 egg, 2 tablespoons of olive oil with salt
Ingredients for the sauce:
– 1 cup of crumbled stale Tuscan bread
– olive oil to taste, powdered or fresh hot red pepper

Preparation:
① Sift the flour into a cone on the breadboard. Form a hole at the center and break the eggs into it, adding the olive oil and a little water if necessary to begin kneading the dough.
② Knead, adding water a little a time, enough to form a firm, even ball.
③ Sprinkle the dough with olive oil, cover it with a clean cloth and set it aside to rest for 30 min.
④ Roll the dough not too thin, cut it in strips about ¼ in. wide and pull each strip of pasta with one hand, holding the other end and rolling it slightly (the correct term is "appicciare") to form rather thick spaghetti 12-13 in. long.
⑤ Flour the "pici" as you go, to keep them from sticking together.
⑥ Cook them in abundant salted water for 5 min., until they rise to the surface, adding a tablespoon of olive oil to the pot to keep them from sticking as they cook.
⑦ Drain the "pici", add them to a pan in which you have prepared a sauce of crumbled bread sautéed in abundant olive oil and hot red pepper and stir well.
⑧ Serve with a sprinkling of grated pecorino.

Another very famous dressing for this type of pasta, also typical of Siena, is "all'aglione" or "all'agliata", that is, a sauce made of tomatoes, hot red pepper, bay leaves and abundant garlic. Classic sauces such as meat sauce, simple tomato sauce and sausage are also used. A "pici" fair is held in Seggiano every August.

🍷 Sovana Sangiovese, Monteregio di Massa Marittima Rosato

Zuppa lombarda (Beans on toast)

Utensils: deep pot, soup dishes
Preparation time: 20 min.
Cooking time: 45 min.
Ingredients for 4-6 persons:
– 1 ¾ lb. of fresh or dried white beans
– 4-6 slices of Tuscan bread
– 2 cloves of garlic
– a few leaves of fresh sage
– 6 cups of cold salted water
– olive oil, salt and pepper

Preparation:
① If using dried beans, soak them overnight before cooking.
② Boil the beans in the water with the garlic, sage and a few tablespoons of olive oil for about 45 min.
③ Place a slice of toasted bread rubbed with garlic in each soup dish and pour the soup over it.
④ Salt, pepper and dribble with olive oil.

🍷 Parrina Rosato

Meat, fish, and side dishes

Paradiso di Pitigliano (Salt cod Pitigliano style)

Utensils: pan, soup tureen
Preparation time: 20 min.
Cooking time: 20 min.
Ingredients for 4/5 persons:
– 1 ¾ lb. of salt cod, already soaked and cleaned
– 5-6 cloves of garlic
– 4 cups of cold water
– parsley, olive oil, salt and pepper
– 6 slices of Tuscan bread

Preparation:
① Rinse the salt cod well to eliminate the excess salt, cut it in medium-sized pieces and place them in a large pan, covering them with cold water.
② Cook on top of the stove, adding the parsley; cook for 15-20 min. until the water comes to a boil.

③ Put the slices of toasted bread, rubbed with abundant garlic, in the soup tureen, cover them with the pieces of salt cod and their cooking broth.

④ Dribble with olive oil and sprinkle with abundant ground pepper.

⑤ Serve in individual soup dishes.

🍷 Bianco di Pitigliano

Cinghiale alla cacciatora (Wild boar hunter's style)

Utensils: pan
Preparation time: 15 min.
Cooking time: 2 hr.
Ingredients for 4-6 persons:
– 2 lb. of fresh wild boar's meat
– 1 onion
– 1 carrot
– 1 can of tomatoes
– 2 cups of white wine
– 2 cloves of garlic
– olive oil
– salt and hot red pepper

Preparation:

① Finely chop together the carrot, onion and garlic; sauté them in the pan with abundant olive oil.

② Add the boar's meat cut in medium-sized pieces and cook for a few minutes until the meat is well browned. Then add a little salt, the hot red pepper and the wine. Let the wine evaporate over high heat for about 20 min.

③ Add the tomatoes and continue to cook over low heat for 1 ½ hr.

④ Serve hot with a dusting of hot red pepper.

🍷 Morellino di Scansano, Brunello di Montalcino, Bolgheri Sassicaia, Chianti Montalbano Riserva

Cipolle alla grossetana (Stuffed onions Grosseto style)

Utensils: deep pot, sharp knife, bowl, pan
Preparation time: 30 min.
Cooking time: 15 min. + 30 min.
Ingredients for 6 persons:

– ½ lb. of ground veal
– 6 large white onions
– 1 fresh sausage
– 1-2 eggs depending on their size
– ⅓ cup of grated parmigiano or pecorino
– ½ cup of vegetable stock (soup cube acceptable)
– ½ glass of white wine
– nutmeg
– olive oil
– salt and pepper

Preparation:

① Peel the onions with the knife (to keep your eyes from watering, peel them under cold running water), then cook them in boiling salted water for 15 min., after having sliced off one end to keep them standing. Drain them and let them cool.

② With the knife, scoop out the inside of the onions, being careful not to break the outside, which must remain intact; retain the onion pulp.

③ Chop the onion pulp and add it in a bowl to the ground veal, the crumbled sausage, the cheese, olive oil, nutmeg, and pepper; salt to taste.

④ Mix well and fill the onion shells.

⑤ Place them in the pan, dampen them with the stock and wine, and cook for 10 min. to evaporate the wine.

⑥ Cover the pan and continue to cook for about 20 min. until the juice has thickened.

⑦ Serve hot accompanied by a mixed salad.

The stuffed onions can also be baked in a pan (350°F), covering the pan with aluminum foil for 20 min. and then continuing to cook uncovered for another 10 min.

🍷 Monteregio di Massa Marittima Novello, Parrina Bianco

Cakes, pies and cookies

Ciaffagnoni (Crêpes)

Utensils: bowl, crêpe pan
Preparation time: 10 min. + 30 min. resting time

Cooking time: 3 min.
Ingredients for 6-8 persons:
– 1 ¼ cup of cake flour type 00
– 4 eggs
– 1 ¼ cup of water
– 2 tablespoons of olive oil
– salt

Preparation:
① With a wire whisk, beat the eggs well with a pinch of salt, then sift into them the flour, a little at a time to keep lumps from forming.
② Add the water, mixing to form a smooth, rather liquid dough. Cover the dough and refrigerate it for about 30 min.
③ Heat the crêpe pan, oiling it with a little olive oil, and pour the batter into it a little at a time, covering the entire surface.
④ Cook well on both sides, turning the "ciaffagnone" delicately.
⑤ Serve with jam, marmalade, Nutella® or sugar alone.

These can also be eaten with a savory filling, such as salami, ricotta and spinach, dusted with grated pecorino, etc.

🍷 Sparkling Bianco di Pitigliano

Sfratto ('Eviction' cookies)

Utensils: pan, breadboard
Preparation time: 1 hr.
Cooking time: 30 min. on top of the stove + 20-25 min. in a moderate oven (350°F)

Ingredients for 4-6 persons for the filling:
– 3 ½ cups of chopped walnuts
– 2 grated orange rinds
– ¾ cup of honey, preferably acacia
– 1 small glass of anise-flavored liqueur
– ⅓ cup of aniseed
– powdered spices (cinnamon, cloves, nutmeg, ginger, pepper)

Ingredients for the dough:
– 2 cups of flour type 00
– ½ cup of sugar
– a pinch of powdered vanilla

– ½ cup of white wine
– olive oil

Preparation of the filling:

① Heat the honey over hot water, being careful not to let it darken, for about 15-20 min.

② Add to the warm honey the finely chopped walnuts, the spices, aniseed and orange rind and cook over low heat to amalgamate well; then add the liqueur, stirring to form a thick paste. Remove the mixture from the heat and set it aside to rest.

Preparation of the dough:

① Mix the sifted flour, sugar and vanilla powder and knead well with the olive oil to form a smooth, even dough.

② Cut the dough and roll it with the rolling pin to form strips not very thick, about 8 in. long and 5 in. wide, dusting them with flour to keep them from sticking.

Preparation of the "sfratto":

① Place some of the honey mixture in the middle of each piece of dough and roll the dough from one end, closing the roll at the other end.

② Press the edges down to keep the filling from seeping out during cooking.

③ Put the rolls on an oven tray covered with buttered and floured oven paper and bake them for 15 min., turning them occasionally to brown them evenly.

④ Slice and serve warm.

🍷 Sparkling Bianco di Pitigliano, Elba Ansonica Passito

LIVORNO AT THE TABLE

The Province of Livorno extends along the Tyrrhenian coast for ninety kilometers and includes the Island of Elba, whose cuisine merits a discourse of its own. Noteworthy among the towns in its territory are the ancient ones of Sassetta and Suvereto – the latter famous for its wild boar festival and its wines – found in the interior zone of the Val di Cornia; and the towns of Castagneto Carducci and Bolgheri, linked not only to the poet Giosuè Carducci, who sang their beauty, but also to such famous wines as **Sassicaia**, **Ornellaia** and **Tignanello**. Interesting for its landscape and naturalist features is the last section to the south of the Etruscan Coast, which includes the *Parco Archeologico di Baratti e Populonia* (Archaeological Park of Baratti and Populonia) where visitors can admire the remains of the ancient Etruscan city, the only one founded on the sea. It is impossible to discuss traditional Livornese cuisine without thinking of a 'multi-racial' influence, deriving from the mingling of races that has distinguished the city of Livorno for centuries. Here, after the issuing of the "Costituzione Livornina" (1593), a declaration guaranteeing religious, commercial and political freedom, there arrived a great variety of peoples from every part of the world, mainly Jews, Muslims, Spanish and Arabs, Greeks, Dutch and English. Although it was founded by the Medici family, who intended to make it an ideal city, Livorno did not develop as a court of the nobility accustomed to sumptuous banquets, but was instead a crossroads of maritime traffic. And for this reason we find today traditional dishes that clearly derive from one or another of the ethnic groups. This is true, for instance of the use of intensely fragrant spices in **cuscussù**, a dish imported from the Arab countries by the Jews; and of **roschette**, a Jewish delicacy made in all of its versions for the Jewish Passover; as well as for the **bolli** and **orecchi di Amman** (Haman's ears) both of which are fragrant cookies.

Obviously, the vicinity of the sea has favored the great quantity and variety of fish that is the main ingredient of many dishes, from starters to main courses. The oysters cultivated in the channel known as the Fosso Reale, when its waters were still clean, were exported all over the world. The Medicean court, in fact, managed to produce them in great quantities (about two hundred thousand a year) to be sent as gifts to the various European sovereigns. There was also a "Casina delle ostriche" (oyster house) in operation up to the 19th century, frequented by many aristocrats, both local and transitory. Today we find scattered throughout the city stalls that sell not only oysters – nowadays imported – but also shellfish of other kinds. The best way to sample them is to eat them raw or dressed with chopped parsley, garlic, spring onion, and anchovies preserved under salt.

Among the starters we also find **frittelline di bianchetti**, **carpaccio di gamberi freschi**, **insalata di polpo** and **acciughe alla povera** or **marinate**, as well as the tasty **cozze ripiene**. One of the first dishes to be sampled without fail is the so-called **carbonara di mare,** which combines the original recipe of the better-known "carbonara" (spaghetti, eggs and cream) with mussels. Then the classic among the most classic seafood dishes, **spaghetti allo scoglio** with fresh seafood and a hint of tomato, in addition to **risotto nero,** a rice dish made with cuttlefish ink.

The fact that Livorno was a port of exchange has favored the entry of new ingredients, and here we need only think of the peppers and tomatoes coming from the New World, which have become the indispensable basis for many recipes (such as the **inno di Garibaldi,** (Hymn to Garibaldi), not to speak of the mingling of habits and customs that the indigenous inhabitants of the territory have adopted as their own. Well-known, in fact, are **stoccafisso** (accompanied by onions and potatoes, but also in many other versions) and **baccalà alla livornese**, the first of which is stockfish, the second salt cod, methods of preserving imported by Basque fishermen in the 16th century. Salt cod is also served **sotto pesto**. **Triglie alla livornese,** mullet cooked with tomatoes, is a delicious specialty. The ready availability of ingredients, however, did not mean an equally rich cuisine for everyone. Only the merchants and the nobility could enjoy it, while the rest of the people tried to manage as well as they could, using a great deal of imagination to create dishes that are often just as rich (in originality if nothing else) with a few, but essential, ingredients, such as the **brodo di sassi** (Stone soup) and **minestra sui discorsi** (Conversation soup). The city underwent culinary expansion toward the inland as well, especially in the last decades of the 19th century, after its importance as a port of trade had begun to decline. It was then that some typical vegetable dishes were created (such as the tasty **patate rifatte**, the **carciofi in tortino** or **ritti** and the **cavolo strasci'ato**) dishes made with potatoes, artichokes and cauliflower respectively) as well as bean dishes (famous is **bordatino**, differing from the Pisan version in that it contains bacon as well as cornmeal, beans, winter cabbage and tomatoes) and meat dishes – mainly based on chicken, rabbit and game – succulent and tasty but at the same time simple such as **coniglio ripieno** (stuffed rabbit) with an omelet of eggs and slices of mortadella.

But the dish that is the unrivaled symbol of Livorno is the delicious but erroneously termed 'fish soup', **cacciucco** with five 'C's' like the minimum variety of fish to be used. A dish that has been at the center of real battles over the improper use of the name, it differs from the Viareggio version in the utilization of more hot red pepper and more fish with bones.

However it may be, apart from this preamble, "cacciucco" is of humble birth, perhaps Turkish (the name is thought to derive from the word "kuciuk" = minute or "kacukli" = tiny bits), the dish of poor people and fishermen, with a very interesting history that dates back to remote times and that seems to reflect the life of the city itself, a crossroads of races and religions. A good "cacciucco", in fact, is made with fish of all kinds, tradition calling for 13 different types, fished according to the season, not expensive but firm and 'meaty', although some declare that the best of all is the one made with prawns, octopus, shrimp, dogfish, scorpion fish and cuttlefish, abundant tomatoes and hot red pepper, to be accompanied by plenty of red wine. One of the favorite snacks of the Livornese, but also an important meal, is **torta di ceci** (chickpea tart, known in Pisa as "cecina"), a sort of wide, thin, crunchy pancake made with water and chickpea flour, baked in the oven in round copper pans. It should be sampled very hot and can be eaten either alone, sprinkled with pepper, or as the filling for a flat, round bun, or the long crusty loaf called "francesino". At times it is served topped with grilled eggplant preserved under olive oil. If you prefer to sample this 'tart' as a sandwich, remember to ask for "un 5 e 5", an age-old expression still used to indicate 5 cents worth of tart and 5 of bread. Scattered around the city, it will not be hard to find the so-called "tortai", pulling the enormous copper pans out of the oven, especially in cold weather. The best of them are however the *Antica torteria al Mercato*, better known as "Gagarin" (Via del Cardinale, no. 24) and the *Seghieri* (Via E. Rossi, no. 19).

As for sweets, the choice is vast, including **frati**, a kind of fried doughnut, and the **schiacciata di Pasqua**, soft and fragrant, as well as simple, inexpensive dishes such as **ricotta briaca**, with ricotta and dried fruit.

During the cold winter evenings it is customary to warm up with the famous **ponce**, a highly fragrant alcoholic drink made with rum and coffee, deriving from the nobler British punch, served very hot with lemon rind (called "vela") in a small glass. There also exists a version "al mandarino", tangerine-flavored, sweeter and not as strong. In summer instead there is the refreshing **persiana** made with anise and mint liqueur, mixed with water.

Elba (*see photo*), being an island, has developed a special culinary tradition, considering both the influence of the presence, albeit brief, of the French entourage of Napoleon Bonaparte during his exile here and the mining activity in the eastern part of the island, which brought in people from elsewhere, as well as the main activity of fishing. Noteworthy among the typical dishes are **sburrita riese**, an exceptionally tasty soup made of salt cod, abundant garlic and hot red pepper, and **gurguglione**, a vegetable stew. Remaining from the Napoleonic interval is **spigola all'imperiale**, bass marinated in red vinegar before being cooked. The Emperor is also said to have adored **seppie co' carciofi** (cuttlefish with artichokes). To be sampled is the particular **schiaccia briaca**, a crunchy, intensely fragrant sweet, while at Easter it is traditional to eat **sportella**, a sweet bread with liqueur and aromatic spices. The island too can boast fine wines such as Ansonica, Aleatico, found also in the heavier version known as Passito, and Elba, also produced as a sparkling wine.

GLOSSARY

Starters, snack, savory pies and luncheon dishes

Acciughe alla povera – Anchovies marinated for days in vinegar and dressed with hot red pepper and raw red onion.

Baccalà sotto pesto – Tasty pieces of salt cod cooked in olive oil and onions, with the addition of pine nuts and raisins, for an incredible combination of sweet and savory flavors.

Frittelline di bianchetti – Whitebait fried in a batter of flour, eggs and water, to be eaten hot sprinkled with lemon juice.

Torta di ceci – One of the most tempting snacks (good also for dinner or supper), made of chickpea flour, water and olive oil. It can be eaten either alone or as a sandwich, but always hot.

Pasta and soups

Bordatino alla livornese – A kind of porridge containing winter cabbage, tomatoes and beans enriched by bacon or filets of anchovies preserved under salt and dissolved in hot olive oil.

Brodo di sassi – Stone soup, a 'poor' recipe that is hard to find nowadays, obviously due to pollution, since it was made in fact with stones taken from the wharf of Livorno, covered with sea herbs, boiled in water to make a broth that was first strained and then used as a soup in which pasta was boiled.

Cacciucco – A dish made with various kinds of fish, both with and without bones, cooked in a long procedure in tomatoes and wine and served on slices of toasted bread rubbed with garlic.

Cuscussù – A recipe from the Arab tradition, made of coarse-grained semolina with veal, lamb and vegetables.

Gurguglione – A sort of stew made of vegetables cooked together, to which is often added fresh tuna, a very good and nutritious dish typical of the summertime cuisine of Elba. Its name derives from an ancient Saracen term indicating a mixture of things.

Inno di Garibaldi – 'Hymn to Garibaldi', an inexpensive dish made with leftover boiled meat and potatoes cooked in a tomato sauce.

Minestra sui discorsi – 'Conversation soup', made of very few ingredients: a veal bone is boiled in water with various herbs; the water is then strained and pasta is cooked in it.

Riso al nero di seppia – A classic risotto made with the ink of squids, flavored with wine and hot red pepper.

Spaghetti di mare – This is a typical seafood dish, whose ingredients must be extremely fresh and highly varied in both quantity and quality – arselle (a kind of small clam), fasolari (a kind of big clam), mussels, etc. – with the addition of shellfish such as shrimp and scampi.

Meat, fish, and side dishes

Baccalà alla livornese – Salt cod soaked in water and cooked in a pan with garlic, onions, tomatoes and red wine, served on slices of Tuscan bread.

Carciofi ritti – Tasty artichokes filled with a mixture of lard, sausage, dried porcini mushrooms and herbs, cooked standing upright in a pan, browned in oil and stock.
Cavolo strasci'ato – A simple dish consisting of cauliflower sautéed and then stewed in tomato sauce. It is found in many cities of the region; in Florence, for example it is made with sausage and black olives.
Cozze ripiene – A succulent dish of mussels filled with ground meat, eggs, herbs and parmigiano, cooked in tomato sauce.
Patate rifatte – Potatoes sautéed in olive oil with chopped sage, garlic and tomato paste.
Sburrita riese – A very tasty stew of salt cod cooked very slowly in a broth containing abundant garlic and aromatic herbs (calamint and thyme) with the addition of hot red pepper. It is served on slices of toasted bread. This was an old recipe popular with miners and fishermen on the Island of Elba.
Seppie co' carciofi – A simple dish made of cuttlefish and artichokes cooked in white wine, with anchovies preserved under salt, garlic and parsley.
Spigola all'imperiale – A delicious recipe for bass, which is marinated in red vinegar for several hours then simmered with herbs (onions, bay leaf and garlic) and served with mayonnaise flavored with garlic and a few drops of white vinegar, or with a sauce "alla maniera francese" (in the French manner) made of finely chopped parsley, garlic, and aromatic herbs

along with a hard-boiled egg crumbled in olive oil, vinegar and mustard.

Tortino di carciofi – A thick omelet made of eggs, artichokes and herbs, which is cooked without turning.

Triglie alla livornese – An appetizing dish of mullet cooked in tomatoes with plenty of garlic and parsley, served on slices of toasted bread.

Zerri sotto il pesto – Small fish that are fried after having been dredged in flour, then placed in a bowl and sprinkled with white vinegar and finely chopped garlic, hot red pepper and olive oil.

Cakes, pies, cookies and liqueurs

Bollo – Cookies of ancient Jewish tradition, usually rounded in shape. Since they are not very sweet, they are good accompanied by jam or cream of various types. Today they are made only rarely.

Frati – Tasty doughnuts made of sweet, fried bread dough, coated in sugar; their name means 'friars', since their shape recalls the tonsure of monks.

Orecchi di Amman – A sweet similar to "cenci", made of fried dough, round in shape, containing few ingredients such as flour, sugar and Vin Santo. The name, which means 'Amman's ears', commemorates the Biblical episode in which Haman, a Persian, wanted to exterminate the Hebrews and take over the Persian kingdom, but was discovered and killed for having plotted against his own king; it is told that his ears were eaten.

Persiana – A thirst-quenching summer beverage made of liqueur flavored with anise and mint mixed with water.

Ponce – A cold-weather drink made of rum "fantasia" (a mixture of alcohol, sugar and scorched caramel to give it color) and coffee, to be drunk with the addition of lemon rind and sugar (try the best in the city at the *Bar Civili*, Via del Vigna, no. 55). A strong and rather particular version is the one called "Torpedine", whose secret ingredients include hot red pepper.

Ricotta briaca – A delicious Christmas cream from the 'poor' Livornese cooking tradition, made of a few ingredients such as ricotta, sugar and chopped hazelnuts or almonds, mixed with a glass of liqueur, giving rise to its name, "briaca", which means 'drunken'.

Roschette – Typical ring-shaped cakes from the Jewish Easter, hard in consistency, very simply made of flour and yeast. There is also a sweet version that calls for eggs and sugar; excellent accompanied by a glass of red wine.

Schiaccia briaca – A very crisp sweet from Elba, traditionally made for Christmas, but now found all year round. It is prepared in round molds with flour, sugar, raisins and dried fruit, flavored with wine.

The surface is sprinkled with sugar and then with Alkermes. Its name (which means 'drunk') derives from the presence of Aleatico wine in the dough. The Elban fishermen always brought a good supply of it with them when they planned to stay out at sea for days at a time.

Schiacciata di Pasqua – A sweet leavened bread baked around Easter, very fragrant, made of sweetened bread dough left to rise for a long time, with the addition of eggs, sugar, orange juice and aniseed. Delicious either alone or with chocolate Easter eggs and a glass of Vin Santo.

Sportella – A typical Elban Easter sweet, made in different versions but always in its characteristic fish shape. It can be found, in fact, either as cookies made of sweetened pie dough or as a ring-shaped loaf of sweet bread flavored with liqueur and aromatic spices. Traditionally, it was the sweet exchanged by fiancés for Easter.

Recipes

Starters, snacks, savory pies and luncheon dishes

Baccalà sotto pesto (Marinated salt cod)

Utensils: glass ovenproof dish
Preparation time: 20 min. + 30 min. resting time
Cooking time: 6 min. for frying
Ingredients for 5/6 persons:
– 1 ¾ lb. of salt cod, cleaned, boned and soaked
– 1 red onion
– 1 handful of pine nuts
– 1 handful of raisins
– white wine vinegar to taste
– 1 bunch of parsley
– 5 tablespoons of olive oil
– flour as required
– oil for frying

Preparation:
① Cut the fish into pieces about 2 in. wide, dust them with flour and fry them in abundant oil. Drain them and place them on paper towels.
② Meanwhile, soak the raisins in hot water.
③ Slice the onions and marinate them in an ovenproof dish with abundant white wine vinegar, until they become translucent. Then drain them and set them aside. Mix the fried codfish, the squeezed and dried raisins, the pine nuts, parsley, olive oil and a few tablespoons of white wine vinegar.
④ Cover and set aside to rest for about 30 min.
⑤ Serve cold as a starter.

🍷 Val di Cornia Vermentino, Elba Bianco

Torta di ceci (Chickpea tart)

Utensils: wire whisk, bowl, pan
Preparation time: 15 min. + 1 hr. resting time
Cooking time: 20 min. in a very hot oven (480°F)
Ingredients for 6-8 persons:
– 2 cups of chickpea flour

– 3 cups of water at room temperature
– 6 tablespoons of olive oil
– salt and pepper

Preparation:

① Sift the flour into a large bowl; add the water a little at a time with a pinch of salt and begin to mix well, avoiding the formation of lumps.

② Cover the mixture and set it aside to rest for 1 hr.

③ Remove the foam that has formed on the surface with a slotted spoon; incorporate 3 tablespoons of olive oil and stir until it forms a cream that is fairly liquid but firm.

④ Grease the pan, pour the mixture into it, adding another 3 tablespoons of olive oil. Bake in a preheated oven for 20 min., checking to ensure that the pan is perfectly level. The tart should be thin, well browned, crunchy around the edges, but still soft.

⑤ Serve hot sprinkled with pepper.

*Tradition has it that this dish was invented by chance at the time of the war between the Pisans and the Genoese in 1284. The Genoese ships, loaded with Pisan prisoners, were caught in a violent storm. The food supplies stored in the hold consisted mainly of sacks of chickpea flour and barrels of olive oil, which, in the confusion, broke and were soaked by seawater, creating a purée that was then salvaged due to dire need and put to dry in the sun, giving rise to this sort of pancake. Upon arriving in port, the Genoese began to cook the mixture, naming it 'gold of Pisa' to commemorate their victory over the city. The "5 e 5" in the form of a sandwich beloved by the Livornese is often enriched with **melanzane sotto il pesto**, slices of eggplant grilled or fried, covered by an abundant mixture of chopped garlic and hot red pepper and sprinkled with vinegar, according to an ancient Spanish recipe.*

Pasta and soups

Cacciucco (Seafood stew)

Utensils: 2 large pans, 1 saucepan, large soup tureen
Preparation time: 30 min.
Cooking time: 2 hr.
Ingredients for 4/5 persons:
– 1 lb. of mussels

– 1 lb. of large clams
– 3 lb. of octopus and cuttlefish, already cleaned
– 12 slices of dogfish or smooth hound
– 10 fish of various kinds: gurnard, scorpion fish, large-scaled scorpion fish, gaper, already cleaned
– 6 mantis prawns
– 4 cloves of garlic
– 1 cup of red wine, 1 cup of water
– 1 ¼ cups of tomato purée
– 3 tablespoons of tomato paste
– a few leaves of fresh sage
– 2 hot red peppers, both fresh and powdered
– olive oil, salt
– 8 slices of toasted Tuscan bread rubbed with garlic
– 1 bunch of parsley

Preparation:

① Leave the clams to purge for several hours in a large pot of cold salted water.

② In the pan, sauté 1 chopped clove of garlic and the sage, then add the wine and after a few minutes the tomatoes, 1 hot red pepper and the octopus cut in small pieces; salt and simmer for about 30 min.

③ Add the cuttlefish cut in small pieces and continue cooking for another 30 min.

④ In the other pan, sauté 1 clove of garlic, then add the tomato paste diluted in a cup of hot water; add the remaining hot red pepper and salt. Add the clams, mussels, mantis prawns and whole fish and simmer for 15 min. If necessary, add another cup of water.

⑤ In the saucepan, sauté 1 clove of garlic and a few sage leaves. Add the dogfish and 1 tablespoon of tomato paste with ½ glass of water, salt and cook over high heat for 15 min.

⑥ In the center of the soup tureen, place the slices of toasted bread, rubbed with garlic and briefly dipped in the fish stew, then proceed as follows: arrange the fish with the clams and mussels on one side of the tureen, the dogfish on the opposite side, and lastly the cuttlefish and octopus in the center on the slices of toasted bread.

⑦ Finish by adding ladlefuls of the liquid stew and a dusting of hot red pepper.

⑧ Serve hot.

This is one of the many, many versions of this hearty fish soup. Some cooks even pass the fish with its bones through a vegetable mill before placing them on the slices of bread.

🍷 Val di Cornia Ciliegiolo, Bolgheri Rosso

Carbonara di mare (Seafood carbonara)

Utensils: deep pot, large pan
Preparation time: 5 min.
Cooking time: that of the type of pasta used
Ingredients for 6 persons:
– 1 lb. of pasta (bavette, linguine or spaghetti)
– ¾ lb. of mussels
– 4 moscardini (tiny octopus)
– 2 cloves of garlic
– 4 extra-fresh egg yolks
– ½ cup of sparkling wine (sparkling white Elba)
– 1 bunch of parsley
– salt and pepper, olive oil

Preparation:
① In the pan, lightly brown the cloves of garlic, add the mussels and moscardini, cleaned and cut into medium-sized pieces. Sauté for a few minutes over low heat. Remove the garlic and add the sparkling wine. Then cover and simmer over very low heat for 10 min., stirring frequently, until the mussels have opened and the moscardini are tender. Remove the mussels from their shells, reserving some of them to garnish the dish, and strain the juices.
② Break the eggs, put the yolks in a large bowl and beat them lightly.
③ Meanwhile, cook the pasta, drain it rapidly and add it to the mussels and moscardini in the pan. Add the eggs and a little of the strained juices and put back over the heat for 2 min., stirring well to amalgamate all of the ingredients.
④ Serve at once with a sprinkling of parsley, a dusting of pepper and a few mussels.

🍷 Val di Cornia Ansonica, Bolgheri Vermentino

Cuscussù (Couscous)

Utensils: 2 deep pots (1 large, 1 medium-sized), 1 wok or similar, 1 large pan, 1 soup tureen, 2 serving dishes

Preparation time: 20 min. for the couscous + 20 min.
Cooking time: 90 min. total
Ingredients per 6 persons:
– 1 ¾ cups of couscous
– 2 lb. of breast of veal
– ¼ lb. of ground lamb
– 1 egg
– vegetables in the quantities preferred (onions, carrots, zucchini, peas, green beans, eggplant, sweet peppers, artichokes, potatoes, celery)
– 2 fresh hot red peppers
– 2 tablespoons of tomato paste
– nutmeg
– ¼ cup of stale bread without the crust
– water or stock (soup cube acceptable) as needed
– olive oil, salt

Preparation:
① In the deep pot, bring the water to the boil with the veal cut in pieces, 1 carrot, 1 stalk of celery, 1 onion and 1 hot red pepper. Simmer for 50 min.
② Remove enough veal stock to equal double the volume of the couscous. Pour it into the other pot and bring to the boil, then sprinkle the couscous into it a little at a time, stirring well with a wooden spoon until it swells but is not too soft in consistency. Pour it into the soup tureen, dust it with pepper and add 1 tablespoon of olive oil; cover and set aside to rest.
③ In the wok, sauté in a little olive oil the vegetables cut in pieces with the hot red pepper and the tomato paste diluted in half a glass of water. Continue cooking until the liquid has reduced.
④ Make meatballs with the ground meat, 1 egg, salt, pepper, 1 pinch of ground nutmeg and the bread dampened in the veal stock and squeezed well.
⑤ Cook the meatballs in a sauce made of tomato paste, onions, parsley and half a glass of water; cook for 10 minutes until the sauce thickens. Then add the meatballs to the vegetables and sauté for a few minutes.
⑥ Fill one serving dish with the boiled meat, the other with the vegetables and meatballs.

⑦ Serve with the couscous dampened with a little of the stock; serve the rest of the stock separately.

🍷 Bolgheri Rosato

Meat, fish, and side dishes

Carciofi ritti (Stuffed artichokes)

Utensils: bowl, deep pan
Preparation time: 20 min.
Cooking time: 20 min. in a moderate oven (350°F)
Ingredients for 4 persons:
– 8 large artichokes or 12 small ones
– 2 oz. of sausage or prosciutto
– 2 cloves of garlic
– 1 bunch of parsley
– 4 tablespoons of olive oil
– salt and pepper
– ½ oz. of dried mushrooms (optional)

Preparation:
① Clean the artichokes, removing the tough outer leaves.
② Cut off the stems so that the artichokes remain standing; press the leaves open and remove any tough fibers inside.
③ With the blender, chop the peeled stems and the bottoms of the artichokes removed, the sausage or prosciutto, the garlic and the parsley (if using dried mushrooms, soften them first in half a cup of warm water). Mix these ingredients well, adding half of the olive oil; add salt and pepper.
④ Fill the cleaned artichokes with this mixture, pressing the leaves open with the fingers (for an even tastier dish, warm the mixture in a casserole over moderate heat for a few minutes, stirring often, before filling the artichokes with it).
⑤ Place the artichokes right side up in an ovenproof pan, adding the other half of the olive oil and a glass of water.
⑥ Cook over low heat for 20-30 min. Baste the artichokes from time to time with spoonfuls of the pan juice.
⑦ Bake in a preheated oven for 20 min.

🍷 Colli dell'Etruria Centrale novello

Cavolo strasci'ato (Brazed cauliflower)

Utensils: deep pot, pan
Preparation time: 20 min.
Cooking time: 10 min. boiling time + 20 min.
Ingredients for 4 persons:
– 2 lb. of cauliflower
– 1 ¼ cups of canned tomatoes
– ¾ cup of pitted black olives
– 3 cloves of garlic
– olive oil, hot red pepper or black pepper
– fennel seed (optional)

Preparation:
① Boil the cauliflower in abundant salted water for 10 min. then cut it in medium-sized pieces and sauté them in hot olive oil with garlic.
② Add the tomatoes, salt and hot red pepper or black pepper (and fennel seed, if desired) and cook for 10 min. Add the olives a few minutes before removing from the heat.
③ Serve hot as accompaniment to meat dishes.

🍷 Val di Cornia Sangiovese

Cozze ripiene (Stuffed mussels)

Utensils: bowl, large pan
Preparation time: 30 min.
Cooking time: 30 min.
Ingredients for 4 persons:
– 24 large cleaned mussels
– 2 eggs
– ¾ lb. of ground beef
– 1 chopped clove of garlic
– mixed chopped herbs (parsley, thyme, basil)
– grated parmigiano
– 4 slices of Tuscan bread cut in half
Ingredients for the sauce:
– ¾ lb. of tomatoes
– 1 carrot
– 1 stalk of celery
– 1 small onion

– 1 glass of water
– salt and pepper

Preparation:

① Open the mussel shells; set the opened mussels aside.

② Mix well all of the other ingredients and fill each mussel shell with some of the mixture.

③ To make the sauce, sauté the chopped vegetables for a few minutes, then add the tomatoes and a glass of water. Adjust the salt, add pepper and cook until the sauce thickens.

④ Add the mussels and cook for 10-15 min.

⑤ Serve with a good sprinkling of pepper and slices of toasted bread rubbed with garlic and lightly dampened in the tomato sauce.

A variation of this dish is made with medium-sized calamari filled with the same mixture, to which are added the finely chopped tentacles; the calamari are then closed with a toothpick. In this case, prolong the cooking time for 20 min.

🍷 Val di Cornia Rosato, Val di Cornia Vermentino

Gurgulione (Stewed mixed vegetables)

Utensils: large deep pan
Preparation time: 20 min.
Cooking time: 25 min.
Ingredients for 6 persons:

– 1 ½ lb. of ripe tomatoes
– 3 large green peppers
– 3 large eggplants
– 3 zucchini
– 1 large onion
– 5 large potatoes
– 1 clove of garlic
– 1 hot red pepper
– 1 bunch of basil, 1 bunch of parsley
– 1 lb. of stale Tuscan bread
– ½ cup of olive oil
– 1 cup of stock (soup cube acceptable)

Preparation:

① Clean, wash and coarsely chop the vegetables.

② Heat the olive oil in the pan with the hot red pepper and

the peeled, crushed garlic. Remove the garlic and add the potatoes first, cooking them alone for about 5 min. Then add all of
the other vegetables and cook for a few minutes over high heat.
Cover the pan, adding a little stock if it is too dry. Simmer over
very low heat until all of the vegetables are done.

③ Serve on slices of toasted bread rubbed with garlic, dressed with
a little chopped basil and parsley and dribbled with olive oil.

*This appetizing side dish is frequently enriched with thick slices of fresh
tuna added to the vegetables for the last 10 min. of cooking time.*

🍷 Bolgheri Rosato

Inno di Garibaldi ('Hymn to Garibaldi')

Utensils: large pan
Preparation time: 20 min.
Cooking time: 40 min.
Ingredients for 4/5 persons:
– 1 lb. of mixed boiled meats (muscle, beef)
– ½ lb. of potatoes
– 2 cups of puréed tomatoes
– 1 clove of garlic
– 1 sprig of rosemary
– olive oil, salt and black pepper (or hot red pepper)

Preparation:
① In the pan, sauté the garlic with the rosemary for a few seconds, then add the puréed tomatoes, salt, cover and simmer over
low heat for 15 min. Add the potatoes, peeled and cubed; continue cooking for 20 min.

② A few minutes before removing from the heat, add the boiled
meat cut in pieces, stirring well to let it absorb the flavors.

③ Serve with a sprinkling of black pepper or hot red pepper.

🍷 Bolgheri Rosato, Chianti Classico

Patate rifatte (Brazed potatoes)

Utensils: large pan
Preparation time: 20 min. soaking time + 20 min.
Cooking time: 30 min.
Ingredients for 6 persons:
– 2 lb. of yellow potatoes

– 2 cups of canned tomatoes (or seeded, peeled ripe tomatoes or 3 tablespoons of tomato paste dissolved in 1 cup of warm water)
– 2 cloves of garlic
– a few leaves of sage
– 1 sprig of rosemary
– olive oil
– salt and pepper

Preparation:
① Peel and cube the potatoes. Place them in a bowl filled with cold salted water and leave them to soak for about 20 min. Drain and dry them with a kitchen towel.
② Sauté the garlic in the olive oil with the finely chopped sage and rosemary for 2 min., then add the potatoes, pepper them and cook over high heat for about 10 min.
③ Add the tomatoes, salt and continue cooking for another 20 min. over low heat. If necessary, add a little water.
④ Serve hot as a side dish for roasted meat.

Scaloppine alla livornese (Veal scaloppine Livorno style)

Utensils: large pan
Preparation time: 20 min.
Cooking time: 15 min.
Ingredients for 4 persons:
– 4 tender, lean slices of veal
– a little butter
– ½ cup of vegetable stock (soup cube acceptable)
– 1 teaspoon of flour
– ½ glass of dry Vin Santo or Marsala
– salt and pepper
– 1 bunch of parsley

Preparation:
① Lightly brown the meat in the pan with the butter. Add 3 tablespoons of stock and cook for 10 min.
② Stir in the flour, the Vin Santo, salt and pepper a few minutes before removing from the heat.
③ Sprinkle with chopped parsley and serve.
🍷 Bolgheri Rosato

Triglie alla livornese (Mullet Livorno style)

Utensils: pan
Preparation time: 20 min.
Cooking time: 20 min.
Ingredients for 4 persons:
– 8 large mullet
– 2 cloves of garlic
– 2 cups of puréed tomatoes
– 1 large onion
– olive oil, salt and hot red pepper, 1 bunch of parsley
– 4 slices of Tuscan bread

Preparation:
① In the pan, cook the tomatoes with the sliced onions and the garlic over low heat for 10 min. Add the cleaned mullet and the hot red pepper and simmer covered over low heat for another 10 min.
② Serve hot with slices of toasted Tuscan bread and a little chopped parsley.

🍷 Val di Cornia Bianco, Suvereto Merlot.

Sburrita (Codfish soup)

Utensils: large deep pot
Preparation time: 20 min.
Cooking time: 90 min.
Ingredients for 6 persons:
– 2 lb. of salt cod already soaked
– 10 cloves of garlic
– aromatic herbs in the quantities preferred (thyme, calamint)
– 1 fresh hot red pepper
– 1 ½ cups of olive oil
– 6 slices of toasted Tuscan bread.
– 3 qt. of water

Preparation:
① In the pot, bring the water to the boil with the peeled and crushed cloves of garlic, the aromatic herbs and the hot red pepper. As soon as it comes to the boil, add the olive oil and cook over medium heat for about 1 hr.
② Cut the codfish into medium-sized pieces, add them to the pot and cook for 30 min.

③ Toast the bread and pour over it the codfish with its broth. Serve hot.

🍷 Elba Bianco

Cakes, pies and cookies

Ciambelle di Pasqua (Easter treats)

Difficulty: easy
Utensils: breadboard, pan
Preparation time: 30 min.
Cooking time: 20 min. in a moderate oven
Ingredients for 6 persons:
– 5 eggs + 1 egg white
– ¾ cup of sugar
– ½ cup of olive oil
– 1 teaspoon of anise
– flour as needed, powdered sugar to garnish

Preparation:
① Mix all of the ingredients on the breadboard, using as much flour as needed to form a firm, even dough.
② Knead the dough for about 20 min., then form ring-shaped cookies 2 in. in diameter. Place them in the greased and lightly floured pan.
③ Brush with egg white and bake for 20 min.
④ Sprinkle with powdered sugar and serve.

🍷 Elba Ansonica Passito, Bolgheri Vin Santo Occhio di Pernice

Frati ('Friar' doughnuts)

Utensils: breadboard, thimble
Preparation time: 20 min. + 2 hr. resting time
Cooking time: 5 min. each.
Ingredients for 6 persons:
– 1 egg
– 8 cups of flour
– ½ cup of olive oil
– 2 tablespoons of sugar
– 1 grated lemon rind

– 1 ¼ cups of water
– 1 cube of brewer's yeast
– seed oil for frying

Preparation:

① Mix and knead the ingredients on the breadboard to form a dough; let it rise for about 2 hr. (it should double in volume).

② Proceed as follows to form the doughnuts: make a ball of dough about 1 in. in diameter, place it on the breadboard and flatten it slightly the palm of the hand. Now press the thimble into the center of the flattened ball of dough to form a hole in the middle.

③ Cover the doughnuts with a cloth and leave them to rest on a table, so that they can rise again.

④ Meanwhile, heat abundant sunflower seed oil in a pan and fry the doughnuts. Drain them and dredge them in sugar while still hot. Serve hot.

🍷 Elba Ansonica Passito

Roschette dolci (Baked cookies)

Utensils: breadboard, oven pan
Preparation time: 20 min. + 40 min. rising time
Cooking time: 20 min. in a moderate oven (350°F)
Ingredients for 8/10 persons:
– 4 cups of flour type 00
– 3 eggs + 1 yolk to garnish
– 4 tablespoons of olive oil
– 4 tablespoons of sugar
– 1 pinch of cinnamon
– 1 teaspoon of orange blossom water or orange-flavored liqueur,
– 1 packet of baking power, 1 pinch of salt
– warm milk as necessary

Preparation:

① Sift the flour into a cone on the breadboard, then add the baking powder and the other ingredients. Knead with enough milk to form a soft but firm dough. Cover and set aside to rest in a cool place for about 40 min.

② Take a bit of dough at a time and roll it with the hands on the breadboard to form a cylinder about ¾ in. thick; cut it in small pieces and form little ring-shaped cookies.

③ Place the cookies on the buttered and floured pan, make 4 oblique slashes on the surface, brush with egg yolk and bake in a preheated oven 20 min.

④ Serve with a glass of sweet wine.

These cookies can also be fried in oil and then dipped in a thick syrup made of water, sugar and cinnamon, cooked for a long time over low heat. The savory version contains no baking powder, but only flour, eggs, olive oil and a little more salt, with the addition of fennel seeds if desired.

Y Elba Ansonica Passito

Schiaccia 'briaca ('Drunken' cake)

Utensils: breadboard, 9 in. round cake pan
Preparation time: 40 min.
Cooking time: 45 min. in a moderate oven
Ingredients for 8/10 persons:
– 8 cups of flour type 0
– 2 ½ cups of sugar
– 1 ⅓ cups of raisins
– 2 ½ cups of chopped nuts (almonds, walnuts, hazelnuts)
– ⅓ cup of pine nuts
– 1 cup of olive oil
– Elba Aleatico red wine as needed
– 1 packet of baking powder
– ¾ cup of Alkermes

Preparation:
① Soak the raisins in ½ cup of Aleatico wine for about 15 min.
② Sift some of the flour onto the breadboard in the form of a cone. Add the baking powder, chopped nuts, raisins, Aleatico, olive oil and ¼ cup of Alkermes.
③ Briefly knead the ingredients together, adding more flour to form a firm, soft dough.
④ Grease the cake pan and line it with oiled paper; grease the paper also and pour in the dough. Sprinkle the top with pine nuts, a handful of unsoaked raisins, ½ cup of Alkermes mixed with 2 tablespoons of olive oil.
⑤ Bake in a preheated oven for 45 min. Serve warm on a large serving dish.

Y Elba Aleatico

LUCCA AT THE TABLE

S trolling through Lucca is like taking a voyage into the past; the very air has a scent of history. Encircled by imposing, still intact Renaissance walls, the city is enclosed in a world without time. Its squares and narrow streets date back for centuries, to Roman antiquity, and everywhere the fascination of ages forever gone seems within hand's reach. The territory of Lucca comprises two rich and densely populated areas, very different from each other, both offering splendid vacations under the sign of nature and good cooking: Garfagnana, the mountainous zone bordering on the Tuscan-Emilian Apennines, where numerous towns are found immersed in peaceful forests that offer enchanting landscapes as well as a wealth of products from the land, such as potatoes and the famous grain called farro; and Versilia on the Tyrrhenian coast, whose major centers – Viareggio, Forte dei Marmi, Pietrasanta and Torre del Lago – offer instead exhilarating entertainment and night life.

During the last few years the province has developed a first-rate response to the tourist demand, especially that of visitors from other countries who are now discovering the beauties of this territory easy to reach and far from the hectic pace of the region's more famous cities. This new spirit of hospitality is evident especially in the rediscovery of the traditional cuisine that can count on the fame of its products, first among the superb olive oil produced in this territory, influenced by both the mountains and the sea. In this part of Tuscany, the contrast between land and sea is very evident; on the one hand we have the mountain tradition, based on inexpensive ingredients linked to the raising of farmyard animals and to the land and the forests, such as chestnuts and mushrooms; while on the coast a truly autonomous cuisine has developed, that of Versilia, based entirely on fish and seafood, raw materials abundantly available. Moreover, up to 1800, just outside the city, in the plain between Viareggio and Lucca, were marshlands that hindered communication between the two areas. Accordingly, we find on the one side of the divide such soups as **pasta e ceci**, **zuppa di cavolo** and the famous **zuppa di farro,** along with the salad called **panzanella del prete** (the richest version of this bread salad with the widest variety of vegetables in addition to prosciutto, pecorino, tuna and hard-boiled eggs). And then **matuffi** made of polenta, simple to prepare but nutritious, often served as a one-dish meal. On the other side we find instead **spaghetti con le arselle**, and **tordelli** – tortelli with a seafood filling, in contrast to those of Lucca, filled with roast beef or pork – and **cacciucco**, which differs from that of Livorno in that it has more shellfish, less bread, and virtually no hot red pepper. We find excellent charcuterie – such as **biroldo**, **buristo**, **prosciutto bazzone** and **tizzone** – frequently accompanied by **pane con le patate** or by **criscioletta**; and then **polpo alla versiliese, fritto misto di paranza** and **grigliata mista**. Here too, as along the entire coastline, are found recipes for the famous **ceè**, baby eels; among them all, the fritters are a must.

The soups of Lucca's inland territory include **garmugia**, a hearty dish made of vegetables and legumes; and then **farinata di cavolo nero** and **polenta di nec-**

cio made with chestnut flour; and among the main dishes, are the appetizing **coniglio alla cacciatora con olive** and **gallina ripiena**. The bread with potatoes typical of Garfagnana (potatoes from Metello are exceptional) keeps longer than traditional Tuscan bread, in addition to being softer and more savory. But it is definitely worthwhile to sample the **schiacciata del cavatore** as well, a kind of bread that was the daily fare of marble miners in the mountainous Alpi Apuane, highly nutritious with its walnuts and "ciccioli" (bits of pork skin and bacon). Another typical food of this territory is **pasimata**, a sweet bread enriched with anise. One of the cheeses produced in the mountains is the so-called **accasciato**, fresh and soft, preferably made with sheep's milk, also known as 'shepherd's dish cheese', which assumes a drooping shape ("accasciato") when unwrapped from its binding. It is at its best when dribbled with the local olive oil and sprinkled with pepper.

Among the sweets typical of the area is the famous **buccellato**, the sweet bread made already by the Romans. Going toward Versilia we find **befanini,** traditional Christmas cookies, and the **dessert Versilia,** a delicious combination of ice cream and sponge cake; and then there is the **torta di farro** of Garfagnana, and the unusual **scarpaccia viareggina**, a sweet-and-savory "focaccia" containing zucchini. Lucca contends with Pisa the origin of the **torta co' bischeri,** or **torta co' becchi**, made of sugar, eggs, cocoa, pine nuts and herbs. Wines hold a place of honor in this part of Tuscany with such DOC denominations as those of Montecarlo and Chianti delle Colline Lucchesi, the perfect accompaniment to every dish, whether fish or meat, from appetizers to desserts. And the Lucchese are always ready to finish their meals with a glass of **Biadina**, an aromatic liqueur with a slightly bitter tang containing mixed herbs and cinchona.

GLOSSARY

Starters, snacks, savory pies and luncheon dishes

Criscioletta – A specialty of Garfagnana made with such inexpensive ingredients as durum flour and cornmeal and cooked in the characteristic "cotte", two disks of steel with two long handles. Excellent when accompanied by bacon and other charcuterie, cheeses, or even eaten alone. In summer, in the days around the feast of St. Lawrence (August 11), one of the most ancient fairs in the territory is dedicated to "criscioletta".

Panzanella del prete – The richer, tastier version of the famous Tuscan salad. Its ingredients include, in fact: radicchio, fennel, carrots, cubes of cooked ham and pecorino, tuna and anchovies preserved in oil, hard-boiled eggs, sweet peppers and capers.

Torta di farro – A savory pie typical of the Tuscan-Emilian Apennines, made of farro, eggs, pecorino, ricotta, aromatic herbs and pepper.

Torta di pepe – A savory pie native to Camaiore. There exist numerous versions, but the most commonly found contains rice, pepper, parmigiano and often beet greens. It is traditionally served around Easter.

Torta salata di patate – Typical of Garfagnana, this savory pie contains potatoes, beet greens, and parmigiano, flavored with nutmeg. Good served warm but even better cold, especially with a topping of lightly whipped cream.

Pasta and soups

Cacciucco versiliese – A delicious meal in one dish that cannot properly be called 'soup', consisting of shellfish, boneless fish, tomatoes and bread.
Garmugia – An ancient savory soup made of vegetables and legumes, ground meat and stock, in vogue among the upper classes of Lucca in the 17th century, and traditionally fed to convalescents for its highly nutritious and tonic powers. It is a real springtime soup, to be made when the main ingredients – asparagus, artichokes, spring onions, fresh peas and broad beans – are at the peak of their natural flavor and freshness.
Spaghetti con le arselle – A simple but tasty first course consisting of spaghetti and arselle (a kind of little shellfish also known as "telline"), in a sauce of fresh tomatoes and garlic.
Tordelli – A sort of square ravioli filled with ground beef or pork, locally made mortadella, beet greens, bread dipped in stock, cheese, eggs and aromatic herbs, to be dressed with meat sauce.
Zuppa di cavolo nero, fagioli e lardo – A cold-weather soup, since it has a high caloric content and calls for winter cabbage, containing Colonnata lard, beans and potatoes.
Zuppa di farro – A soup made with one of the most ancient cereals, recently rediscovered and used in many recipes, both sweet and savory. Here it is made with chopped sautéed onions, carrots and celery, enriched with lard and beans.

Meat, fish, and side dishes

Coniglio alla cacciatora con olive – A tasty main course typical of the countryside, but easily found along the coast as well, made of rabbit meat flavored with tomatoes, finely chopped aromatic herbs and olives.
Fritto misto di paranza – A classic of many restaurants that prepare this dish depending on what the fishing boats have brought back that morning. The various types of fried fish include anchovies, little codfish, mullet, sole, calamaretti, and so on, which are simply dusted with flour and fried. The "paranza" is a type of fishing boat used to catch smaller fish not far from the shore.
Gallina ripiena – A hearty rural recipe for hen stuffed with a mixture of beef, parmigiano, bread dipped in milk, aromatic herbs and eggs. It can be cooked in vegetable stock or in a large pan with garlic and oil.

Triglie con fave, pomodori e basilico – A tasty, simple recipe that combines the savor of the sea with that of the land, its ingredients being mullet and fresh broad beans, cherry tomatoes and basil.

Cakes, pies, cookies and liqueurs

Benzone – A sweet popular in Garfagnana since the time it was ruled by the Duchy of Modena, made by a simple recipe calling for flour, eggs, sugar, raisins and candied fruit.

Biadina – An aromatic liqueur with a slightly bitter tang containing herbs mixed with cinchona. Pine nuts are dropped into the glasses in which it is served. Its curious name derives from the fact that it was invented during the times of cattle fairs by the proprietor of a shop that sold goods of all kinds, including "biada", feed for horses, who was accustomed to offer his customers a glass of his alcoholic creation.

Buccellato – A sweet bread typical of Lucca made with eggs, yeast, flour, sugar, raisins and milk, flavored with aniseed. Of ancient Roman origin, its name is thought to derive from its elongated mouth shape (*bucca*). In medieval times it was the traditional gift to the feudal lord, and was even mentioned in a document from the 15th century. Later it became the custom to give it as an omen of good luck. This delicious, enticingly scented sweet can also be used to prepare other desserts such as *Zuppa lucchese*: slices of "buccellato" sprinkled with Vin Santo and covered with liquid cream, whipped cream and fresh strawberries.

Budino di farro dolce – A pie made of cream of farro in a pastry shell.

Dessert Versilia – A velvety ice cream created in the Roaring Years – the fashion-crazy 1960s in Versilia – made of sponge cake, cream, chocolate, liqueur and zabaglione, it is sold in characteristic small jars (*Gelateria Artigiana Versilia*, Via Francalanci, no. 14, Bozzano-Massarosa, Lucca).

Pasimata – Typical of Easter, the day on which it is brought to church to be blessed, this is a sweet bread enriched with anise; while in the Garfagnana version, eggs, sugar and raisins are also added and it is flavored with Vin Santo and lemon rind.

Scarpaccia viareggina – A sweet-and-savory pie made with such simple ingredients as sugar, eggs and zucchini, popular among seamen on the Versilia coast, who gave it its name because when cooked it had the same thickness as the sole of an old shoe.

Torta d'erbi o co' becchi – A sort of sweet pie in a piecrust shell, with a filling of wild herbs (today substituted by beet greens or spinach), flour, eggs, sugar, chocolate, raisins and pine nuts. It owes its unusual name to the way the edges are formed, by pinching, very much as in the Pisan "bischeri".

Torta garfagnina – Cake made of almonds, flour, and eggs, flavored with anise and lemon, typical of the mountainous zones.

Recipes

Starters, snacks, savory pies and luncheon dishes

Torta di pepe (Pepper pie)

Utensils: breadboard, rolling pin, deep pot, bowl, 10 in. round pie pan
Preparation time: 30 min. + 30 min. resting time for the dough
Cooking time: 40 min. in a moderate oven
Ingredients for pie dough for 6 persons:
– 2 cups of flour type 0
– ½ cup of softened butter
– 1 whole egg
– water as required
– 1 pinch of salt
– breadcrumbs as required

Preparation:
① Sift the flour onto the breadboard in the form of a cone, then add the butter, egg and salt. Knead, adding enough water to form a firm dough. Cover the dough and set it aside to rest in a cool place for about 30 min.
② Roll the dough very thin with the rolling pin and place it in the pie dish, which has been previously buttered and dusted with breadcrumbs.

Ingredients for the filling:
– 1 ⅔ cups of Carnaroli rice
– 2 cups of milk
– 2 cups of water
– 4 whole eggs
– 2 oz. of grated parmigiano
– 2 oz. of grated pecorino
– a pinch of nutmeg
– abundant powdered black pepper, salt

Preparation:
① Cook the rice in a pot with the milk and water, being careful not to overcook it; drain and set aside to cool.
② In a bowl, beat the eggs with the salt, grated cheese, nutmeg and pepper.

③ Stir and mix well until the mixture is soft and fluffy. Pour it into the pie shell, leveling the surface and sprinkling it with more pepper.

🍷 Colline Lucchesi Bianco

Torta salata di patate (Savory potato pie)

Utensils: large bowl, ovenproof pan or dish
Preparation time: 30 min.
Cooking time: 20 min. in a preheated moderate oven
Ingredients for 8 persons:
– 2 lb. of yellow potatoes
– ½ cup of boiled beet greens or spinach
– 2 oz. of grated parmigiano
– 1 ¾ oz. of grated pecorino
– 1 egg
– milk as required
– 1 clove of garlic
– 1 tablespoon of butter
– 1 bunch of chopped parsley
– 1 sprinkling of nutmeg, salt and pepper, breadcrumbs as required

Preparation:
① Put the potatoes in a pot of cold water, bring to the boil and cook for 30 min. (if using a pressure cooker, for 15 min. after the whistle starts to blow). Peel them and mash them with a potato masher directly in the bowl. Add the vegetables, squeezed and chopped, the egg, the aromatic herbs, spices and salt; add the milk slowly, stirring to form a soft, even mixture.
② Butter the pan, sprinkle it with the breadcrumbs, removing the excess, and pour the potato mixture into it. Level the surface, sprinkle it with more breadcrumbs and bake.
③ Serve warm.

🍷 Colline Lucchesi Bianco

Pasta and soups

Garmugia (Meat and vegetable stew)

Utensils: large pan
Preparation time: 30 min.

Cooking time: 50 min.
Ingredients for 6 persons:
– ½ lb of ground veal
– 4 oz. of diced bacon
– 4 small onions or 1 bunch of spring onions
– 1 ½ cups of fresh green peas
– 4 artichokes cut in slices
– ¾ cup of asparagus tips blanched in boiling water
– 1 ½ cups of fresh broad beans
– 1 clove of garlic
– 5 cups of vegetable stock (soup cube acceptable)
– olive oil, salt and pepper
– toasted Tuscan bread

Preparation:
① In the pan, brown the bacon and sliced onions in olive oil for a few minutes. Then add the ground meat and stir to let it absorb the flavors. Add the beans and the other vegetables (it is preferable to blanch the asparagus first) and sauté them for a few minutes.
② Add the stock, bring to the boil and simmer over very low heat for about 40 min., until the vegetables and beans are done.
③ Serve the stew with toasted bread cubes, a dribbling of olive oil and a sprinkling of pepper.
🍷 Montecarlo Rosso

Tordelli (Filled pasta)

Utensils: breadboard, rolling pin, food mill, deep pot, pan, bowl, pasta cutter
Preparation time: 45 min.
Cooking time: 5 min.
Ingredients for pasta dough for 6 persons:
– 4 cups of flour type 0
– 2 whole eggs
– milk as required
– salt, 1 tablespoon of olive oil

Preparation:
① Sift the flour on the breadboard to form a cone, then add the eggs and salt and knead well.

② Roll the dough with the rolling pin into long, thin strips; flour them to keep them from sticking, and set them aside to rest while preparing the filling.

Ingredients for the filling:
– ½ lb. of ground pork
– ½ lb. of ground beef
– ½ lb. of ground veal
– 1 sausage
– 1 ⅔ cups of beet greens or spinach
– 3 ½ oz. of parmigiano
– 2 eggs
– ½ cup of white wine
– 1 ladleful of vegetable stock
– soft inside of 1 small bread roll soaked in milk
– 1 tablespoon of tomato paste
– 1 pinch of nutmeg, salt and pepper

Preparation of the tordelli:
① Cook the beet greens or spinach in abundant salted water. Drain them, let them cool, chop them coarsely and place them in a bowl.
② In a saucepan, sauté the garlic, parsley, rosemary and thyme in a little olive oil. Add the ground meat and the sausage; brown them, then add the wine. Let the wine evaporate, then add the tomato paste and the stock. Cook until the sauce thickens.
③ Remove from the heat, cool slightly and pass through the food mill. Add the beet greens to the meat mixture; add the bread, well squeezed and crumbled, the eggs, parmigiano, hot red pepper, nutmeg, and salt, and mix well.
④ Place a little of the filling at regular distances in the center of each strip of pasta. Then fold the pasta in half to cover the filling, pressing it down with the hands around each bit of filling, and cut it with the pastry cutter. Press the edges of the tordelli with a fork. Continue until all of the ingredients are used, flouring the tordelli to keep them from sticking.
⑤ Bring to a boil abundant water in a pot and cook the "tordelli" a few at a time. As they rise to the top, lower the heat and scoop them out with a sieve or slotted spoon.
⑥ Serve dressed with abundant meat sauce and parmigiano.

🍷 Montecarlo Rosso, Colli di Luni Vermentino

Meat, fish, and side dishes

Triglie con fave, pomodori e basilico (Mullet with broad beans, tomatoes and basil)

Utensils: frying pan, pan, bowl, serving tray
Preparation time: 20 min.
Cooking time: 2 min. in the frying pan + 4 min. in a moderate oven (350°F)
Ingredients for 4 persons:
– 8 fillets of mullet
– 1 ½ cups of fresh broad beans
– 3-4 ripe tomatoes
– a few leaves of basil
– olive oil, salt, pepper

Preparation:
① Salt the fish fillets and brown them lightly in a frying pan with a little oil. Then put them in a hot oven for 4 min.
② Dice the tomatoes, discarding the seeds, and place them in a bowl; add the hulled broad beans and sprinkle with salt, pepper and olive oil.
③ Arrange the fish filets on the serving tray and cover them with the tomatoes and the broad beans.
④ Garnish with a few basil leaves and serve.

The Livornese version also calls for celery and parsley.

🍷 Montecarlo Bianco, Colline Lucchesi Sauvignon

Cakes, pies and cookies

Budino di farro ("Farro" pudding)

Utensils: 2 deep pans + 9 in. round pan
Preparation time: 45 min.
Cooking time: 1 hr. in a moderate oven (350°F)
Ingredients for 6 persons:
– readymade pie dough
– 1 cup of "farro" from Garfagnana
– 1 ¼ cups of milk, 1 pinch of salt
Ingredients for the cream:
– 2 egg yolks +1 whole egg

– 1 ¾ cups of powdered sugar
– ½ cup of flour
– 2 cups of milk
– 1 lemon rind
– ¾ cup of sheep's milk ricotta
– ¼ cup of liqueur (Strega or Maraschino or rum)

Preparation:
① Simmer the milk with the farro and a pinch of salt over low heat until all of the milk has been absorbed, stirring frequently to keep it from sticking.
② To make the cream, put the milk, sugar, eggs, flour and lemon rind in a pot and bring to the boil over low heat, stirring constantly to keep it from sticking.
③ Remove from the heat, remove the lemon rind and incorporate the sieved ricotta, the liqueur and the cooked farro. Mix well, slowly and thoroughly.
④ Butter and flour the pan, line it with the pie dough, pour in the creamy mixture leveling the surface, and bake for one hour.
⑤ Serve the pudding with a dusting of powdered sugar.

🍷 Colline Lucchesi Vin Santo Occhio di Pernice

Scarpaccia viareggina (Zucchini cake)

Utensils: soup tureen, 9 in. round cake pan
Preparation time: 20 min.
Cooking time: 1 hr. in a moderate oven
Ingredients for 6 persons:
– 1 ⅓ lb. of zucchini
– 1 ½ cups of flour type 00
– ¾ cup of sugar
– 2 eggs
– ¼ cup of butter melted over hot water
– 1 packet of vanilla flavoring
– half a glass of milk
– a pinch of salt, olive oil

Preparation:
① Make a batter with the sifted flour, the sugar, eggs, butter, vanilla flavoring, warm milk and salt. Stir it well and incorporate the very finely chopped zucchini.

② Pour the mixture into a buttered and floured cake pan; dribble it with olive oil and bake for 1 hr. Serve hot.

🍷 Colli Lucchesi Bianco, Montecarlo Vin Santo

Torta garfagnina (Garfagnana cake)

Utensils: bowl, saucepan
Preparation time: 30 min.
Cooking time: 60 min. in a low oven (300°F)
Ingredients for 6 persons:
– 2 cups of flour
– ¾ cup of sugar
– ⅓ cup of butter
– ½ cup of hulled almonds
– 3 eggs
– 3 tablespoons of rum
– 1 teaspoon of aniseed and 1 tablespoon of milk
– ½ cube of brewers yeast
– grated rind of an organically grown lemon
– 1 pinch of salt, powdered sugar to garnish

Preparation:
① Plunge the almonds into boiling water for a few seconds, drain and peel them, then dry them well and chop finely.
② In a bowl, mix the sifted flour with the sugar, almonds, lemon rind, pinch of salt and aniseed.
③ Melt ¼ cup of butter over low heat; let cool and mix with the other ingredients, adding the rum and the eggs. Stir well to form a smooth, even mixture; then add the yeast dissolved in the warm milk.
④ Grease the pan, pour the mixture into it and bake for 1 hr.
⑤ Serve dusted with powdered sugar.

🍷 Montecarlo Vin Santo Occhio di Pernice

MASSA AND CARRARA AT THE TABLE

The Alpi Apuane on one side and the sea on the other give this territory a highly varied culinary tradition. Although the two cities of Massa and Carrara are distinct, clearly demarcated urban centers, their cooking traditions are both influenced by their shared Etruscan origins, closely linked to farming and rural life as well as to marble mining in the quarries. And due to their closeness to the sea, fish has been widely used to create such special dishes as **ravioli di mare** (pasta in the traditional ravioli shape, but filled with boiled fish, usually spigola, sea bass or cod, blended and dressed with garlic and parsley) or delicacies such as salt cod and stockfish; while sheep-farmers have developed the famous breed called the **pecora di Zeri**, as well as lamb, **agnello**. Moreover, the picturesque inland territory of the Lunigiana still shows evidence of the importance it had in the remote past as well as in Roman times, and even more in the Middle Ages, when its towns and castles were true centers of power. And through this region there also passed a section of the renowned Via Francigena, traveled by pilgrims from northern Europe on their way to Rome already in the 10th century. This territory, striding the mountains between Tuscany and Liguria, is very interesting as regards gastronomy, because it has absorbed and reinterpreted flavors of different origin, transforming them into a tradition of its own, one of great renown.

A highly important role is held by flour of various types used to prepare both humble pasta dishes such as **testaroli** and richer ones such as "gnocchi" and "pappardelle" made of chestnut flour; along with various polenta dishes, such as the delicious **polenta Ficca** with vegetables and beans or the **cazalà** and **mataluffi** of Carrara, of thinner consistency, the former dressed with mushroom sauce, the latter with olive oil and parmigiano; as well as white polenta with rabbit, dressed with seasonal ingredients. Reigning supreme among the cereals is rice, used to prepare many first courses, such as **bomba di riso**, and as the main ingredient of savory pies, sweets and "frittelle" such as **frisoli**.

Then there are **patate di Zeri**, used in the tasty soup known as **frascadei**, and **cipolle di Treschiet**; other vegetables and the typical fruit of the territory, such as the particular **mela rotella**, as well as the wild herbs used as filling for the **torta d'erbi** in all its variations. The woods that grow in the inland area offer products of the highest quality such as mushrooms – foremost among them porcini, and then the rare "cavazza" with its intense flavor – and chestnuts, the basic ingredient of simple, appetizing recipes such as **moglo**, a sort of thin polenta pancake cooked on chestnut leaves in the typical "testi", to be eaten with ricotta, or **gnochi mes'ci**.

Many other dishes as well are cooked in that curious utensil called the *testo*, of ancient Etruscan origin, made of cast iron or clay or terracotta. They are commonly used in a pair, and are formed of two round plates, heated under the glowing ashes of a fire, on which are cooked directly "focacce", **testaroli**, polenta, and **panigacci**, as well as meat such as lamb, and potatoes. Foods cooked with these utensils have a texture midway between the crunchiness of those baked in the oven and the softness of those cooked over steam.

Among the various ancient specialties that have survived to our own day are dishes of charcuterie such as **biroldo** – a fine sausage for true gourmets, made of pork, spices and blood – **filet** and **mortadella** from Lunigiana, and **spalla cotta** from Filattiera; but over them all reigns supreme the aromatic **lardo di Colonnata IGP**, placed in brine with aromatic herbs, spices and salt in marble basins rubbed with garlic and left to season for at least three months. Game too holds a place in the traditions of this area.

The cheeses of Lunigiana, such as "caciotta" and pecorino, are well known, like its ricotta, ideal as appetizers but equally perfect as dessert, accompanied by the finest honey.

Sweets and breads of different kinds find ample space in this cuisine, prepared on festive occasions by traditional procedures in jealously guarded recipes still handed down through the generations, such as the delicious **amor di Pontremoli**, the **spongata di Pontremoli** and the **carscenta**. Among the breads to be sampled is **pan Marocco,** of a distinctive dark colour, with olives; and the equally fragrant **Marocca di Casola** made with chestnut flour, wheat flour, milk and potatoes.

The multiplicity of dishes allows only a broad overview of what this land can offer, and even the recipes given are only a small part of what can be found.

Last but not least are the wines, which find here the ideal setting for accompanying dishes from appetizers to desserts. Outstanding among them are those of the Colli Apuani and those of Lunigiana, in particular the Val di Magra and Colli di Luni.

The town of Fivizzano is famed for the production of **Amaro Clementi**, also called "Elixir China", made of cinchona and medicinal herbs mixed according to the same ancient recipe since 1884.

GLOSSARY

Starters, snacks, savory pies and luncheon dishes

Arbadela – Savory pie baked in the oven, highly aromatic insofar as it contains wild fennel, and tasty thanks to cornmeal, onions, beet greens (the ancient recipe called for wild herbs), parmigiano and ricotta.

Barbotta – A tasty timbale made of wheat grain and vegetables, either zucchini flowers or Treschietto onions, as preferred.

Focacette di Aulla – Small, flat loaves of leavened wheat flour and cornmeal cooked in the traditional "testi", rounded in shape with a diameter of about 6 inches, eaten with charcuterie and cheeses.

Panigacci – Unleavened bread of very ancient origin, made of wheat flour, water and salt mixed to form a rather liquid batter, cooked briefly in the typical "testi" and eaten either dressed simply with olive oil or filled with charcuterie or cheese, preferably soft ones like "crescenza" or "raveggiolo".

Torta d'erbi – A savory pie containing beet greens, ricotta, eggs and parmigiano. In the past it was made with wild herbs gathered in the fields and underbrush.

Torta di riso alla Montignoso – A tasty rice pie typical of the Easter season, made of rice and eggs, parmigiano and milk, flavored with cinnamon, nutmeg and pepper.

Pasta and soups

Cazalà – A rather thin polenta, dressed with meat sauce or mushroom sauce.

Frascadei – A tasty, nutritious soup well suited to cold weather, made with winter cabbage, potatoes and wheat flour dressed with a mixture of chopped lard, parsley and mortadella. Its name derives from the leafy stems of the winter cabbage.

Mataluffi – Similar to *Polenta cazalà*, but differing in the dressing, which consists of olive and grated cheese.

Gnochi mes'ci di castagne – Rectangular-shaped gnocchi made of chestnut floor, excellent dressed with butter and fresh sage, or olive oil and grated pecorino.

Lasagne bastarde – A kind of pasta typical of Lunigiana, irregular in shape, dark in color and sweetish in flavor, made of chestnut flour and wheat bran. The lasagne are coarsely cut and usually cooked in layers alternating with tomato sauce and lard or sausage; or without tomatoes and with abundant pecorino alone.

Polenta 'Ficca' – A succulent dish that calls for long preparation, made of puréed Borlotti beans, white and yellow cornmeal, and a wide variety of herbs and vegetables: from Savoy cabbage to nettles, from pumpkin to borage, passing though potatoes and tomatoes, and then enriched with lard. Its name derives from the fact that the slices of polenta were "ficcata" (stuck into) the vegetables. It should be sampled on site, due to the difficulty in procuring the ingredients, which must be extra fresh.

Polenta incatenata – A simple, nutritious soup made of 'poor' ingredients found growing wild in the fields (herbs), cornmeal, black-eyed peas, potatoes, cabbage and parmigiano, It is called "incatenata" (chained together) because these ingredients are bound with olive oil and cheese.

Testaroli – This simple, typical dish, which may date back to Roman times, is a sort of primordial pasta made of water and flour mixed to form a batter and cooked on "testi". The disks of pasta are then cut into diamond shapes, plunged into a pot of boiling-hot water, but with the heat off, for a few minutes, drained and dressed in various ways, ideally with pesto but also with olive oil and pecorino or with porcini mushroom sauce.

Today it is not easy to find *testaroli* cooked in the ancient way, since it calls for a large fireplace, the right kind of wood and "testi" made of a special kind of terracotta that is no longer made, as well as housewives patiently bending over the fire to keep it at the right temperature. *Testaroli* are sometimes served dressed with parmigiano or pecorino and olive oil.

Meat, fish, and side dishes

Agnello di Zeri con patate – The Zerasca sheep is a hearty breed, of medium size, with very tender flesh, almost sweet to the taste but with a decided aroma. Ideally, it is cooked on "testi", but is also good fried.

Bomba di riso – This specialty can easily serve as a meal in one dish. It consists of a rice pie baked in the oven, filled with stewed quail or pigeons. Since it calls for the use of game, it is best eaten locally, also because its name indicates the preparation of the recipe, a 'bomb' made of boiled rice dressed with eggs, butter, parmigiano, onions and various herbs.

Polenta bianca con coniglio – A dish of corn flour polenta accompanied by stewed rabbit.

Cakes, pies, cookies and liqueurs

Amor di Pontremoli – Delicious mouthfuls formed of two crunchy wafers with a cream filling of delicate, indescribable flavor, the original recipe for which is a jealously guarded secret.

Carscenta della Lunigiana – A cake flavored with anise containing sugar, flour, milk, butter, cream, raisins and pine nuts whose dough is left to rise for a long time. Boasting a long tradition handed down from generation to generation, its original recipe is not known for certain, as regards quantities, rising time and cooking time. This cake, made by the ancient recipe, can be sampled at the chestnut fair held in the Commune of Comano.

Ciorchiello di Casette – A soft, anice-flavored sweet shaped like a medium-sized doughnut, giving rise to its name, which means 'circular', and dark in colour, which keeps for weeks thanks to its consistency. The long, elaborate procedure for making it and letting it rise ensures its conservation, and in fact it was a food that the marble miners took with them into the quarries. In local tradition, the *Ciorchiello* was used as a gift of good omen during the Easter period and was blessed in church on Palm Sunday.

Frisoli – Appetizing rice fritters sprinkled with sugar, eaten both as snacks and as dessert with a glass of good Vin Santo.

Focaccia carrarina – A round, flat loaf about 6 in. in diameter, dark brown in color, made with hazelnuts, almonds, raisins, anise and walnuts mixed with flour and sugar to form a dough that is left to rise naturally for a long time. Once baked on feast days, it can now be found all year long.

Marocca di Casola – An ancient round loaf of bread baked in a wood-burning stove, dark brown and intensely scented with chestnuts and potatoes, its main ingredients. A fair dedicated to it is held on the last Sunday in October at Casola, the town where it originated.

Pan Marocco – Bread with a golden crust, made of wheat and corn flour, with black olives, flavored by the addition of garlic, hot red pepper, rosemary and sage. It is baked in round loaves with diameter of about 9 in. in a wood-burning stove over chestnut leaves, and is typical of the olive-picking season (November-December).
Its name derives from its particular color, linked by the local people to the inhabitants of Morocco.

Spongata – A sort of pie of ancient tradition, formed of two disks of pastry of amber-gold color. It was made during Carnival time and given as a pledge of love by a fiancé to his future bride. Its preparation is long and elaborate, calling for the use of strictly locally grown ingredients. It is a delicacy to be sampled without fail, for its aromatic scent and its equally fragrant creamy filling containing honey, nuts, candied fruit, bread and a secret mixture of spices.

Torta Cybea – An ancient, delicious sweet made of chestnut flour and marrons glacés, round in shape and dark in color. Its dough also contains honey, candied fruit and spices. It is baked on the occasion of the "Quintana Cybea", a historical re-evocation of the 16th century that is held on the first weekend in August, created at the time when the city of Massa was founded in 1557. It is named for the ancient family of Cybo-Malaspina, lords of the city for many years.

Torta di riso dolce carrarese – A fragrant cake made of rice, eggs, milk and liqueur, either rectangular or round in shape, formed of a bottom layer of rice and a top layer of cream that when cooked takes on its distinctive caramel-brown colour. It is usually baked for March 19, St. Joseph's Day.

Torta Pasqualina alla Massese – A sweet rice cake typical of the Easter period, made of rice, eggs and milk.

Recipes

Starters, snacks, savory pies and luncheon dishes

Arbadela (Savory cheese pie)

Utensils: colander, bowl, 12-13 in. round baking pan
Preparation time: 20 min. draining time + 20 min. preparation time
Cooking time: 30 min. in a moderate oven (350°F)
Ingredients for 6 persons:
– 3 lb. of spring onions
– ¾ lb. of beet greens
– 3 ½ cups of corn flour
– 1 cup of ricotta
– 3 ½ oz. of grated pecorino
– a handful of wild fennel
– a glass of milk
– olive oil
– pepper
– salt

Preparation:
① Coarsely chop the onions with the beet greens and fennel and put them in a colander, adding the salt; let them drain for about 20 min.
② Place the drained vegetables in a bowl with the flour, cheese, pepper and ricotta. Mix well, adding olive oil, until the dough is soft and fluffy.
③ Lastly, add the glass of milk.
④ Spread the dough in a greased pie pan, brush it with olive oil and bake in a preheated moderate oven for 30 min.
⑤ When the crust is golden, remove the pie from the oven and serve cut in squares, either hot or cold.

In a more highly flavored version of this cake, the first step is varied by boiling the beet greens, draining them, squeezing them and then chopping them fine. In the meantime, lightly sauté the onions in a pan for a few minutes with butter and a little olive oil, then proceed as described above, starting from step two.

🍷 Colli di Luni Rosso, Candia dei Colli Apuani Amabile

Barbotta (Savory zucchini pie)

Utensils: bowl, square baking pan
Preparation time: 15 min.
Cooking time: 45-50 min. in a moderate oven (350°F)
Ingredients for 4 persons:
– 8 cups of flour
– 1 ½ lb. of zucchini flowers
– 5 tablespoons of olive oil
– 1 glass of water
– olive oil
– salt, pepper
– butter

Preparation:
① Make a dough with the flour, oil, salt and warm water.
② Clean the zucchini flowers and plunge them briefly into boiling salted water. Chop them fine and add them to the mixture. Stir until the dough is smooth and even.
③ Butter the pan and pour in the dough, leveling and oiling the surface. Bake in a preheated oven for 45-50 min.
④ Cut into large pieces and serve hot.

This dish exists in a second, even tastier version: 2 ½ cups of corn flour, 2 glasses of milk, 1 onion, 3 tablespoons of olive oil, 2 oz. of parmigiano with the onion.

🍷 Candia dei Colli Apuani Secco, Parrina Rosato

Torta d'erbi (Cheese and vegetable pie)

Utensils: bowl, deep pan (wok type) and 9-11 in. round cake pan
Preparation time: 30 min.
Cooking time: 45 min. in a moderate oven (350°F)
Ingredients for 6-8 persons:
– 4 lb. of beet greens
– 1 cup of ricotta
– 2 eggs
– pecorino
– a few breadcrumbs
– 1 clove of garlic
– olive oil, salt and pepper
– 2 rolls of ready-made pie dough

Preparation:

① Clean the vegetables, chop them, parboil them in salted water for two minutes and then lightly sauté them in a pan with a little olive oil and garlic.

② In a bowl, mix the vegetables well with the ricotta, eggs, pecorino, breadcrumbs, a pinch of pepper and a little olive oil.

③ Grease the cake pan, place a sheet of oven paper in it and line it with the first round of dough.

④ Spread the mixture over the dough and cover it with the second round of dough, pressing the edges together.

⑤ Brush the surface with oil and prick it with a fork to keep the crust from swelling.

⑥ Bake in a hot oven for about 45 min.

⑦ Serve cold.

If homemade pie dough is preferred, make it as follows:
– 1 ½ cups of flour
– ½ cup of water,
– 3 tablespoons of olive oil, salt

① Sift the flour into a bowl and add the salt, olive oil and water. Mix the ingredients well to form a smooth, compact dough.

② Divide it in half and roll it very fine with a rolling pin to form two disks about 10-12 in. round.

In the past this pie was made with wild herbs such as borage, wild fennel, sow thistle, salad burnet, lamb's lettuce, dandelion and many others that today only a few lucky persons can still find growing in the fields. To make it even tastier, sauté the vegetables with a crumbled sausage or with diced Colonnata lard.

🍷 Candia dei Colli Apuani sparkling Bianco, Val di Magra Bianco

Crostini al lardo di Colonnata (Lard on toast)

Utensils: pan
Preparation time: 20 min.
Cooking time: 5 min. in a hot oven
Ingredients for 4 persons:
– ¼ lb. of Colonnata lard sliced thin
– 8 medium-thick slices of Tuscan bread
– 2 cloves of garlic
– olive oil

– salt and pepper

Preparation:

① Toast the slices of bread for a few minutes and rub them with garlic.

② Place the slices of lard on them and heat in a hot oven for 5 min. until the lard melts.

③ Sprinkle with pepper and serve hot.

🍷 Colli dell'Etruria Centrale Rosso Novello or Rosato, Colli di Luni Rosso

Torta di riso alla Montignoso (Savory rice pie Montignoso style)

Utensils: 12 in. round pan, deep saucepan, large bowl

Preparation time: 20 min.

Cooking time: 30 min. in a hot oven

Ingredients for 4 persons:

– 1 ⅔ cups of rice, type Baldo, Balilla or Roma
– 3 eggs
– 3 tablespoons of olive oil
– 1⅓ cup of milk
– 3 ½ oz. grated parmigiano
– cinnamon
– nutmeg
– pepper, salt to taste
– a few breadcrumbs
– a little butter

Preparation:

① In a pot, boil the rice in salted water; drain it when half cooked and rinse it with cold water to stop the cooking process.

② Beat the eggs in a bowl and add the rice, cheese, olive oil, milk, a little cinnamon and salt.

③ Butter a pan and spread the breadcrumbs evenly over the bottom and sides, to keep the rice from sticking as it cooks; turn on the oven.

④ Pour the rice mixture into the pan and bake it in the oven.

⑤ Remove the pie from the oven as soon as it turns golden brown. Cut it in wedges and serve it hot or cold, either alone or with vegetables or a green salad.

🍷 Colli di Luni Vermentino Bianco, Parrina Rosato

Pasta and soups

Gnochi mes'ci (Gnocchi)

Utensils: breadboard, deep pot
Preparation time: 30 min.
Cooking time: 15 min.
Ingredients for 4 persons:
– 4 ¾ cups of flour
– 3 ¾ cups of chestnut flour
– warm water as required
– pecorino or parmigiano
– ½ cup of olive oil
– salt and hot red pepper to taste

Preparation:
① Sift the two kinds of flour together onto a breadboard, add the warm water and mix to form an even dough.
② Roll the dough not too thin, to a thickness of about ¼ in. Cut it in rectangles of about 2 × 1 in. and dust them with flour to keep them from sticking.
③ Plunge the gnocchi into salted boiling water one at a time; cook them about 15 min. over low heat.
④ Drain and dress with cheese, olive oil and hot red pepper to taste.

🍷 Colline Lucchesi Rosso

Polenta incatenata ("Bound" polenta)

Utensils: large deep pot
Preparation time: 1 night soaking time for the beans, 30 min.
Cooking time: 90 min.
Ingredients for 4 persons:
– ½ lb. of dried Borlotti beans
– 2 ½ cups of fine-grain corn flour
– 1 lb. of winter cabbage
– 1 fresh hambone
– parmigiano
– 3 qt. of salted water
– olive oil
– salt and pepper

Preparation:

① Soak the beans overnight with a teaspoon of baking soda to soften the skins.

② Place the hambone in the pot with the water for about 30 min. Add the beans and cook for 15 min.

③ Clean the winter cabbage and cut it into strips. Add it to the pot along with half a cup of olive oil, and continue to cook for another 30 min.

④ Remove the bone and begin to sprinkle in the flour slowly, stirring to keep lumps from forming.

⑤ Simmer for another 45 min. to obtain a thick, soft cream. If it seems too dry, add a little more water.

⑥ Serve in individual soup bowls with a dribbling of olive oil and abundant cheese.

Some cooks use black-eyed peas instead of beans, and add potatoes; however, this is a recipe in which all of the ingredients blend harmoniously together. Precooked beans can also be used to save time.

🍷 Colli di Luni Rosso

Lasagne bastarde (Chestnut and wheat flour lasagna)

Utensils: deep pot, pan, breadboard and rolling pin
Preparation time: 20 min. + 1 hr. resting time for the pasta dough
Cooking time: 30 min. for the sauce, 5 min. for the lasagna
Ingredients for pasta dough for 4 persons:
– 1 ¾ cups white flour
– ¾ cup of chestnut flour
– 1 cup of warm water
– salt to taste

Ingredients for sauce for 4 persons:
– 3 pork sausages
– 1 medium-sized can of tomatoes
– 1 carrot
– 1 onion
– ½ glass of red wine
– grated pecorino
– olive oil
– salt

Preparation:

① Sift the two kinds of flour together onto a breadboard, add the water and knead to form a firm, even dough.

② Roll the dough very fine with a rolling pin or pasta machine. Place it on a kitchen towel and let it dry for about 1 hr.

③ Meanwhile prepare the sauce. Sauté the finely chopped carrot and onion; as soon as the vegetables are golden brown, stir in the crumbled sausage and continue to sauté over medium heat. Add the tomatoes and let the sauce simmer for about 30 min.

④ Cut the pasta dough into diamond shapes about 1 ½-2 in. per side and cook them at once in boiling salted water with a tablespoon of olive oil for 5 min; plunge them into the pot one at a time to keep them from sticking.

⑤ Drain the lasagna and place them in an ovenproof dish, alternating with layers of sauce. Sprinkle with pecorino and serve hot. Otherwise, brown the dish for 10 min. under the grill.

If the lasagna is to be eaten a few days later, let it dry a little longer. In this case, all of the lasagna may be plunged into the pot at the same time.

They can also be dressed only with olive oil and abundant pecorino and browned in the oven for 15 min., or with a sauce made of leeks, lard and tomatoes.

🍷 Parrina Rosato, Colli dell'Etruria Centrale Novello Rosso

Meat, fish, and side dishes

Agnello di Zeri con patate (Lamb with potatoes)

Utensils: oven pan
Preparation time: 20 min.
Cooking time: about 1 hr., depending on the size of the leg of lamb, in a moderate oven (350°F)
Ingredients for 4-6 persons:
– 1 boned leg of lamb, about 5 lb.
– 2 cloves of garlic
– 1 ¾ oz. of Colonnata lard sliced medium thick
– 2 lb. of potatoes
– rosemary, sage, bay leaf

– olive oil, salt and pepper
– white wine (optional)

Preparation:

① With a sharp knife, cut little slits all over the leg of lamb.

② Peel the potatoes and cut them in medium-sized pieces; place them in a pan.

③ Finely chop together a mixture of lard, garlic, sage, salt, pepper and rosemary. Insert it in the slits cut in the meat.

④ Salt and pepper the meat again and place it in the pan with the potatoes, dribble with olive oil, add the bay leaf and a little white wine (optional).

⑤ Roast in a moderate oven for about 1 hr. Lamb should be cooked very slowly to keep it from becoming dry and stringy.

The best way to prepare this recipe would be first to procure lamb and potatoes grown at Zeri, and then 'testi' in which to cook the dish over glowing coals, so that the meat and potatoes are crunchy on the outside and tender on the inside.

🍷 Carmignano Rosso

Stoccafisso con le patate alla carrarina (Stockfish with potatoes Carrara style)

Utensils: pan
Preparation time: 30 min.
Cooking time: 30 min.
Ingredients for 4 persons:
– 1 ½ lb. of soaked stockfish
– 2 lb. of potatoes
– 4 ½ cups of puréed tomatoes
– 1 onion
– 2 cloves of garlic
– a few fillets of salted anchovies, rinsed
– ½ glass of white wine
– olive oil
– salt, parsley and hot red pepper

Preparation:

① Clean the stockfish well and cut it in rather large pieces.

② Peel the potatoes and cube them.

③ In a pan, sauté the anchovies and finely chopped herbs in olive oil; when they are golden brown, add the pieces of fish. Stir and cook for a couple of minutes.

④ Add the white wine, let it evaporate, then add the tomatoes. Simmer for 10 min., then add the potatoes.

⑤ Cook over low heat until the sauce thickens.

⑥ Serve in individual dishes, accompanied by plain polenta if desired.

🍷 Vernaccia di San Gimignano, Colli di Luni Vermentino

Patate con i funghi porcini (Potatoes with porcini)

Utensils: pan
Preparation time: 25 min.
Cooking time: 25-30 min.
Ingredients for 4 persons:
– 6 large potatoes
– ½ lb. of extra-fresh porcini mushrooms
– 2 cloves of garlic
– olive oil
– 1 sprig of rosemary
– 1 sprig of thyme
– salt, pepper

Preparation:

① Peel the potatoes, wash them, cut them in wedges and soak them in salted water for 15 min.

② In a pan, sauté the peeled and crushed garlic in olive oil.

③ Drain the potatoes, dry them with a clean cloth and add them to the pan for about 10 min.

④ Meanwhile clean the porcini mushrooms delicately without washing them but using a damp cloth. Cut them in slices about ⅓ in. thick.

⑤ Add the mushrooms to the potatoes, stir and cover until the mushrooms have wilted. Continue cooking without a cover for another 10-15 min.

⑥ Serve as accompaniment to grilled or roasted meat.

This is a typical dish to be cooked under "testi" covered in ashes in the ancient manner.

🍷 Colli dell'Etruria Centrale Novello Rosso, Chianti Rufina Vivace, Colline Lucchesi Rosso

Cakes, pies and cookies

Frittelle di castagnaccio (Chestnut flour fritters)

Utensils: deep pot, pan
Preparation time: 10 min.
Cooking time: 5 min.
Ingredients for 4 persons:
– 3 ¾ cups of chestnut flour
– water or milk as required
– oil for frying
– a pinch of salt
– fresh sheep's-milk ricotta

Preparation:
① Mix the flour with the water or milk, avoiding lumps; add a pinch of salt and mix well to form a batter.
② Drop tablespoonfuls of batter into sizzling hot oil and fry them a few at a time, turning to brown them well.
③ Drain them on paper towels and sprinkle with ordinary sugar or powdered sugar.
④ Serve hot topped with ricotta.

🍷 Aleatico dell'Elba, Pomino Vin Santo Bianco Amabile

Torta pasqualina alla massese (Easter cake)

Utensils: deep pot, bowl, 9 in. round cake pan or ceramic oven-proof pan
Preparation time: 40 min.
Cooking time: 90 min. in a moderate oven
Ingredients for 6-8 persons:
– 4 cups of whole milk
– 12 whole eggs
– 1 ⅔ cups of rice, type "Originario" or "Balilla"
– 1 ½ cups of sugar
– 1 packet of vanilla flavoring
– ½ cup of liqueur type "Strega" or "Grand Marnier"
– rind of a lemon or an orange
– butter
– powdered sugar
– a pinch of salt

Preparation:
① Boil the rice in salted water, drain it and let it cool, stirring to keep it from sticking.
② Boil the milk and let it cool.
③ Beat the eggs with the sugar and vanilla flavoring in a bowl.
④ Add the milk a little a time, the lemon or orange peel, the liqueur and lastly the rice, mixing well.
⑤ Butter the cake pan, fill it with the rice mixture and bake for 1 ½ hr. until the surface of the cake is golden brown and a toothpick stuck into it comes out dry.
⑥ Let the cake cool, sprinkle it with powdered sugar and serve.

This is one of many versions of this recipe. If preferred, it can be enriched by adding raisins softened in liqueur and pine nuts.

🍷 Moscadello di Montalcino, Candia dei Colli Apuani Bianco Amabile

PISA AT THE TABLE

P isa, a city of very ancient origin occupying a strategic position at the mouth of the Arno, boasts a great tradition as a powerful maritime Republic that once dominated the Mediterranean as far as the gates of Asia Minor. In the 13th century it was conquered by the Genoese and was later encapsulated in the dominions ruled by Florence and the Medici, who thus acquired a gateway to the sea and turned the city into an important university centre, a tradition that still survives today. The Valdarno area is now an important center for the processing of leather, some of very high quality, used to make wearing apparel as well as shoes and handbags.

Pisa's rich heritage of art makes it one of the most famous Italian cities and a destination for tourists from all nations. Its Leaning Tower, standing in the magnificent Piazza dei Miracoli is one of the world's best-known postcard images. Its territory ranges from the sea to inland areas stretching as far as Volterra and its surroundings, one of the classic landscapes of the Tuscan countryside.

Although Pisa has been influenced by other cities and in particular by Florence, due to its long domination, it has managed to keep unaltered its culinary tradition, not particularly elaborate, but featuring simple recipes made of humble but genuine ingredients, based mainly on fish and seafood that, thanks to Pisa's maritime trade, have been enriched by flavors and tastes through the introduction of precious spices such as saffron, nutmeg, cloves, coriander and others. With many Mediterranean countries from France to Morocco, but especially with Livorno, it contends the origin of the famous **farinata di ceci**, here called **cecìna**, which was once used as a substitute for bread.

Seafood dishes reign supreme in the city's restaurants, with the savory **riso alle arselle** and **bavettine col pesce**, the **minestra di pesce**, and then the so-called **cèe alla pisana**, a sort of frittata of tiny baby eels with a very particular taste, today replaced by whitebait since they are now protected by law. The list continues with nutritious, tasty dishes such as **stoccafisso con le patate**. And then there are soups such as the one called simply **di pane**, a bread soup that when cooked again becomes "ribollita", but here is eaten fresh, with seasonal vegetables and home-style bread – outstanding is the one baked in the town of Montegemoli – or **bordatino** made with winter cabbage, polenta and beans.

The inland parts of the territory offer rural dishes such as **trippa alla pisana con le erbe**, and specialties with game such as **piccioni alla S. Miniato**, as well as refined ones such as those containing the **tartufo bianco** of S. Miniato, a truffle of pungent odor and almost spicy flavor, typical of the autumn period – found for only three months a year, it is highly prized – which adds a distinctive touch to many dishes ranging from the simplest scrambled eggs to the most elaborate stuffed rabbit. An important national truffle fair is held in November.

A special kind of cake, which is also made in other parts of the region but which originated here, is the **torta coi bischeri**, typical of the Easter season, in both savory and sweet versions, the former containing rice and spinach, the latter rice again, but accompanied by cocoa and sweetened with raisins and candied fruits.

Special mention is due the **ciliegie** of Lari, a town just outside Pisa that markets more than twenty varieties of cherries both fresh and in the form of jam, to which one of the most important springtime fairs of this region is dedicated.

Cheeses too are noteworthy, among the best the pecorino produced around Migliarino and S. Rossore, mostly soft in texture, excellent either fresh or aged, to be accompanied by honey in all its varieties or included in recipes for other dishes to heighten their delicate flavors.

In recent years this area has also become important for its production of wines: **Chianti dei Colli Pisani** and **Bianco Pisano di S. Torpè** with the relevant Vin Santo and **Montescudaio**, all ideal companions to dishes made of fish, meats both white and red, game and cheese.

GLOSSARY

Starters, snacks, savory pies and luncheon dishes

Cecìna – A flat savory pie made of chickpeas, to be eaten at any hour of the day, sprinkled with pepper, found everywhere in the classic food shops.

Torta coi bischeri salata – A savory pie typical of springtime and the Easter season in general, made with rice, beet greens and spinach. Pisa contends its origin with Lucca, where it is made without rice and is called *Torta coi becchi*.

Pasta and soups

Bavettine sul pesce – A delicate dish made of fish and seafood, very fresh and summery, served with pasta of the "bavetta" type, and truly fabulous when made with fresh fish.

Bordatino alla pisana – A sort of liquid polenta, an ancient dish typical of the humble daily fare of seaman, made of corn flour, garlic and tomatoes, nowadays enriched with winter cabbage, pumpkin and beans.

Minestra di pane – A rural dish of ancient origins containing winter cabbage, pumpkin, beans, herbs and stale Tuscan bread.

Minestra di pesce alla pisana – A tasty dish that was frequently prepared by fisherman in the past.

Minestra sullo scio di Volterra – A very simple soup of humble origin, consisting of sautéed chopped garlic and rosemary added to water, olive oil and a few canned tomatoes, in which egg pasta is cooked, to be served hot with parmigiano.

Pasta e ceci alla pisana – A hearty first course made of pasta and chick peas, some of which are left whole while the others are mashed into a cream, flavored with tomatoes, hot red pepper and rosemary.

Ravioli al tartufo – A simple, classic dish containing ricotta and spinach, ideal for savoring the fragrance and particular taste of the local truffles.

Risotto con le arselle – A risotto containing arselle (a kind of small clam), with a delicious taste and aroma

Meat, fish, and side dishes

Cèe alla pisana – A typical festive dish since it was prepared only for special occasions due to its refined nature and high cost. In the past it was made with tiny baby eels, called "cèe" ("cieche", i.e. blind ones) that were found at the mouths of rivers and were widely used in the cuisine of Livorno as well. They are now protected by law, but it is possible to find this very special kind of "frittata" made with tiny just-hatched fish from certified fish-farms, or with whitebait.

Cinghiale alla Volterrana – A sumptuous dish made of wild boar's meat, stewed with tomatoes, wine, olives and herbs and accompanied by polenta.

Stoccafisso con le patate – A meal in one dish, unique and nutritious, consisting of stockfish and potatoes, typical fishermen's fare since stockfish was easy to transport and preserve in long voyages at sea.

Trippa alla pisana con le erbe – A hearty dish made of tripe dressed with tomatoes and herbs such as parsley, sage, bay leaf, basil, mint and thyme.

Cakes, pies, cookies and liqueurs

Biscotti all'olio e vino – Simple, tasty cookies made with commonly used ingredients such as olive oil and wine.

Kinzica – A baked sweet known as "Brutto buono ai pinoli" (ugly but good with pine nuts) in spherical shape, made of dough containing pine nuts and sprinkled with powdered sugar of particular flavor. The dough must be kneaded for a long time. Its name is linked to that of the Pisan princess who saved the city from being invaded by Saracen pirates in the 15th century.

Torta coi bischeri dolce – A sweet version consisting of a pastry shell filled with a mixture of cocoa, rice, raisins, candied fruits and pine nuts. Its name derives from the fact that leftover curls of short pastry are placed as decoration around the circumference, forming little curls resembling the keys on violins, in Tuscan dialect called "bischeri". This cake, like its savory twin, is traditionally offered guests at Easter dinner.

Torta pisana – A very particular pie made of a bottom layer of pie dough and a top one of pasta dough, filled with marzipan, very fragrant since it contains sweet liqueur; outstanding is the one made by the pastry shop *Federico Salza* (Borgo Stretto, no. 46).

CRISTOFORO MUNARI, *Still Life with Fruit, Glassware, Porcelain and Ladyfingers*, Florence, SPSAD, Uffici del Soprintendente (detail)

Recipes

Starters, snacks, savory pies and luncheon dishes

Tartufo sul pane (Truffles on bread)

Utensils: frying pan
Preparation time: 10 min.
Cooking time: 5 min.
Ingredients for 4 persons:
– 2 oz. of white truffles from S. Miniato
– 1 tablespoon of grated parmigiano or pecorino
– 1 clove of garlic
– 4 slices of Tuscan bread type Montegemoli
– 1 tablespoon of breadcrumbs
– olive oil, salt and pepper
– 1 ladleful of vegetable stock (soup cube acceptable)

Preparation:
① In a frying pan, heat the oil with the garlic for a few minutes, without letting it burn. Remove the garlic and add the truffles sliced very fine; salt to taste.
② Stir in the breadcrumbs, cheese and a ladleful of stock.
③ Let evaporate over high heat for a maximum of 2 min.
④ Toast the slices of bread and spread them with the truffle mixture.
⑤ Dust with pepper and serve hot.

The white truffle was known already in medieval times, and was considered to possess aphrodisiac powers. Today it can be picked only by "tartufai", authorized truffle hunters governed by a strict discipline that even specifies marketing regulations. This area also holds two Guinness records, one for the biggest truffle ever found (over 5 lb.) and a more recent one for the truffle sold for the highest amount (an amazing 330,000 dollars) at public auction.

🍷 Bianco Pisano di S. Torpè

Pasta and soups

Bordatino alla pisana (Vegetable and polenta soup)

Utensils: large deep pot, food mill, saucepan
Preparation time: 15 min.

Cooking time: 2 hr.
Ingredients for 6-8 persons:
– 1 lb. of winter cabbage
– 1 ⅔ cups of dried Cannellini (or Borlotti) beans
– 1 ½ qt. of the water in which the beans have cooked plus a few beans passed through the food mill
– 2 ½ cups of corn flour
– ½ lb. of pumpkin
– 2 carrots, 2 stalks of celery
– 1 onion, 3 cloves of garlic
– 2 tablespoons of olive oil
– 2 tablespoons of tomato paste
– parsley, salt and hot red pepper
– grated pecorino

Preparation:
① Soak the beans overnight, then cook them in 2 qt. of salted water.
② Finely chop the vegetables and the garlic. Sauté them in a saucepan along with the tomato paste.
③ Clean, wash and coarsely chop the winter cabbage and the pumpkin.
④ Pass some of the beans through the food mill; return them to their cooking water and bring it to the boil.
⑤ Add the sautéed vegetables, stir and add the cabbage and pumpkin. Cook covered for 15 min.
⑥ Lastly, sprinkle in the corn flour, stirring frequently to keep lumps from forming. Simmer for about 1 hr.
⑦ Serve with a dusting of hot red pepper, a dribble of olive oil and pecorino.

Bordatino, *whose name may come from the fact that this polenta soup was frequently consumed aboard ships, was a dish commonly prepared by fishermen along the Tuscan coast, with some variations from one area to another in the original recipe, which called only for cornmeal, tomato paste and sautéed garlic. In Livorno, in fact, it was usually enriched by the addition of bacon, or by fillets of salted anchovies dissolved along with the garlic in sizzling hot oil. To save time, precooked beans can be used, discarding the liquid in which they are preserved.*

🍷 Montescudaio Rosso, Chianti delle Colline Pisane Bianco

Minestra di pane (Bread soup)

Utensils: large deep pot (preferably terracotta)
Preparation time: 10 min.
Cooking time: 130 min.
Ingredients for 4 persons:
– 1 lb. of stale Tuscan bread
– 1 ⅔ cups of Borlotti beans
– 2 stalks of celery
– 2 carrots
– ½ lb. of pumpkin
– 2 zucchini
– 1 onion
– 5-6 ripe tomatoes
– parsley
– 1 soup cube, olive oil, salt and pepper

Preparation:
① Soak the beans overnight, then cook them in 2 qt. of salted water.
② Finely chop the vegetables and sauté them in abundant hot olive oil.
③ Add the cooked beans and a little of their cooking water; simmer for about 2 hr.
④ Place the slices of toasted bread, rubbed with garlic (optional) in individual soup plates and pour the soup over them.
⑤ Serve dribbled with olive oil and dusted with pepper.

This is one of the most ancient 'poor' soups in Tuscan tradition, when housewives put in the pot whatever they happened to have on hand. It was in any case a one-dish meal designed to fill the stomach for hours, and thus highly nutritious and loaded with calories. From this recipe originated the more famous "ribollita", which was re-cooked the day after with the addition of stock or simply water and a few more vegetables, if available.

🍷 Montescudaio Rosso

Minestra di pesce alla pisana (Fish soup Pisan style)

Utensils: large deep pot, large pan, blender, soup tureen
Preparation time: 20 min.
Cooking time: 40 min.

Ingredients for 6-8 persons:
– 2 ½ lb. of fish, both saltwater varieties (turbot, anchovies, mullet, gurnard, etc.) and freshwater varieties (trout, eels, tench, etc.)
– 1 ½ qt. of water
– 4 cloves of garlic
– 1 onion
– 1 stalk of celery
– 2 ripe tomatoes
– 1 carrot
– finely chopped parsley
– rind of one lemon
– crust of parmigiano
– 10 tablespoons of olive oil, salt
– 6-8 slices of toasted bread rubbed with garlic

Preparation:
① Clean the fish and cut them in large pieces.
② Boil the vegetables with the lemon rind and the crust of parmigiano in water for about 20 min.
③ In a pan, sauté the crushed garlic in olive oil, add the fish and cook over medium heat for a few minutes, stirring. Add this mixture to the stock; salt, pepper and simmer for another 20 min.
④ Drain the fish, remove any remaining bones, set aside a few whole pieces and blend the rest in the blender for a few seconds.
⑤ Place the slices of bread in the soup tureen and pour the soup over them, decorating it with chopped parsley.

A specialty of the fishermen at the mouth of the Serchio – the river on the boundary between the provinces of Pisa and Lucca – where there was abundant fish, both saltwater and freshwater varieties, which were combined in perfect harmony in this dish.

🍷 Val di Cornia Rosato, Colli dell'Etruria Centrale Novello

Minestra sullo scio di Volterra (Sizzling soup Volterra style)

Utensils: deep pot, saucepan
Preparation time: 10 min.
Cooking time: 30 min.
Ingredients for 4-5 persons:
– ⅔ lb. of dried egg pasta (type "quadrucci", tagliatelle broken into small pieces)

– 2 cloves of garlic
– 2 ripe or canned tomatoes
– 2 sprigs of rosemary
– 4 cups of boiling water
– olive oil, salt and pepper
– grated parmigiano or pecorino

Preparation:

① Boil the water with a little salt, pepper and the tomatoes cut in pieces.

② In a saucepan, sauté the sliced garlic and the rosemary in 3 tablespoons of olive oil. When golden brown, add them to the pot of water.

③ Add the pasta and cook as indicated for the type used.

④ Serve with a dribbling of olive oil and a sprinkling of parmigiano.

The name of this very simple, tasty soup derives from the fact that, when the sautéed herbs are added to the water, it emits a particular sizzling sound.

🍷 Pisano di S. Torpè Bianco

Pasta e ceci alla pisana (Pasta and chickpeas Pisan style)

Utensils: food mill, deep pan
Preparation time: 15 min.
Cooking time: 25 min.
Ingredients for 4-5 persons:
– 2 cups of cooked or canned chickpeas
– ⅔ lb. of pasta, trenette type
– a few sprigs of rosemary
– 2 cups of vegetable stock (soup cube acceptable)
– 2 tablespoons of tomato paste
– 3 cloves of garlic
– parsley, olive oil, salt and hot red pepper

Preparation:

① Finely chop the garlic and sauté it in the pan with a little rosemary, hot red pepper and a pinch of salt for about 2 min. Add the tomato paste diluted in a little water, and simmer over moderate heat.

② Pass most of the chickpeas through the food mill, leaving a small quantity whole.

③ Add them to the pan with the sautéed mixture, dampening with stock if necessary, and bring to the boil.

④ Add the pasta and cook for about 10 min.

⑤ Serve in soup dishes with a sprinkling of hot red pepper and 1 sprig of rosemary.

🍷 Colli dell'Etruria Centrale Bianco, Val di Cornia Rosato

Ravioli al tartufo (Ravioli with truffles)

Utensils: deep pot, pan
Preparation time: 5 min.
Cooking time: 3 min. + 2 min.
Ingredients for 4 persons:
– ⅔ lb. of ravioli filled with ricotta and spinach
– 1 ½ oz. of truffles
– 2 tablespoons of butter
– 1 tablespoon of cooking cream
– 2 tablespoons of parmigiano
– ¼ cup of nutmeats (optional)
– salt and pepper

Preparation:
① In the pot, bring to a boil abundant water for cooking the ravioli.
② Melt the butter with the cream in a pan, grate some of the truffles into it, add salt and pepper. Chopped nutmeats can also be added if desired.
③ Plunge the ravioli in the boiling water, add salt and cook for 3 min.
④ Drain the ravioli and lightly sauté them in the pan, stirring and turning to let them absorb the sauce.
⑤ Serve the ravioli in soup dishes with a sprinkling of parmigiano and one of grated truffles.

🍷 Colli di Luni Vermentino

Risotto alle arselle (Rice with arselle)

Utensils: 1 large pan
Preparation time: 10 min. + 1 hr. soaking time for the arselle
Cooking time: 5 min. + 15 min.
Ingredients for 6 persons:
– 1 ½ cups of rice

– 2 lb. of fresh (or frozen) arselle (can be substituted with small clams)
– finely chopped mixture of parsley and 2 cloves of garlic
– 2 cups of small fresh tomatoes, cherry or piccadilly type
– 4 cups of vegetable stock (soup cube acceptable)
– 1 teaspoon of butter
– ½ cup of water, olive oil, salt and pepper

Preparation:
① Leave the arselle to soak for 1 hr. in the kitchen sink filled with cold salted water, to remove the sand. Frozen arselle need only be rinsed well.
② In a large pan, place 1 whole clove of garlic and the arselle, cover and simmer over moderate heat for about 5 min. until the shells open; remove the garlic along with any arselle that have failed to open.
③ Strain the liquid left in the pan and set it aside.
④ Remove the shells from the arselle, leaving a few of them whole to garnish the dishes.
⑤ Briefly blend the fresh tomatoes to a coarse consistency.
⑥ Finely chop 1 clove of garlic with the parsley and lightly sauté the mixture in a pan with the butter and 4 tablespoons of olive oil. Add the shelled arselle and sauté for 2 min., then add the tomatoes and lastly the rice. Dampen with the arselle cooking water and let it evaporate.
⑦ Add more of the hot vegetable stock and cook over moderate heat for about 15 min., depending on the type of rice.
⑧ Remove the risotto from the heat, stir and turn it with a teaspoon of butter for a few minutes. Serve with abundant pepper, garnished with a few of the arselle left in their shells.

🍷 Montescudaio Bianco, Vernaccia di San Gimignano

Meat, fish, and side dishes

Trippa alla pisana con le erbe (Tripe with herbs Pisan style)
Utensils: large pan
Preparation time: 15 min.
Cooking time: 40 min.
Ingredients for 6 persons:
– 2 lb. of veal tripe already boiled

– ¼ lb. of sliced bacon or lard
– 1 bunch of fresh herbs (parsley, sage, bay leaf, basil, mint, thyme, fennel, oregano, calamint)
– 1 stalk of celery, 1 carrot, 1 onion, 2 cloves of garlic
– 1 cup of puréed tomatoes
– ½ cup of white wine
– a few tablespoons of grated parmigiano or pecorino
– olive oil, salt and pepper
– 4 cups of vegetable stock (soup cube acceptable) if necessary

Preparation:
① Rinse the tripe, drain it well and cut it into strips.
② Clean, wash and finely slice the vegetables; finely chop the garlic.
③ In the pan, sauté the garlic and bacon in olive oil for 3 min., then add the tripe. Braze with white wine and let it evaporate for a few minutes.
④ Add the puréed tomatoes and the bunch of herbs; salt, pepper and cook for 30 min. If it becomes too dry, add a little stock.
⑤ Continue cooking until the tripe is done and well amalgamated.
⑥ Serve hot with abundant parmigiano and pepper.

🍷 Colli di Luni, Montescudaio Rosso

Cakes, pies and cookies

Torta co' bischeri (Rice pie)
Utensils: 2 large bowls, breadboard, 10-12 in. round cake pan
Preparation time: 30 min. + 1 hr. resting time for the pie dough
Cooking time: 45 min. in a hot oven (400°F)
Ingredients for 6-8 persons:

For the pastry:
– 2 ½ cups of flour type 00
– 3 egg yolks
– ¾ cup of sugar
– ⅔ cup of butter
– 1 lemon rind
– ½ cup of anise flavored liqueur type "Sambuca"
For the filling:
– ¾ cup of rice

– 3 ½ oz. of unsweetened chocolate
– 3 cups of milk
– 2 eggs
– ⅓ cup of sugar
– 1 ½ tablespoons of butter
– ½ cup of pine nuts, ¼ cup of raisins, ¾ cup of candied fruit
– 1 lemon rind
– 1 pinch of salt, 1 of cinnamon, 1 of nutmeg

Preparation of pie dough:

① Mix well in a bowl the softened butter, egg yolks, sugar, flour, lemon rind and glass of liqueur. Knead well and set aside to rest for 1 hour.

Preparation of filling:

① Cook the rice in the milk with a pinch of salt, then let it cool well.

② Place in a bowl the egg yolks, sugar, liqueur, softened butter, coarsely grated chocolate, and the rice; mix well.

③ Whip the egg whites until stiff and fold them gently into the rice mixture. Add the raisins, candied fruits and pine nuts.

Preparation of the pie:

① Spread the pie dough on the breadboard. Butter the pan and line it with the dough, pressing it down well and setting aside the excess amount. Prick it with a fork to keep it from swelling while baking, then put it in a hot oven for a few minutes to dry a little.

② Fill it with the rice mixture and level the surface. With the leftover pastry dough, make strips and place them around the edge of the pie dish, pinching them with the fingers to form a fluted edge. Bake the pie for about 45 min.

This pie has very ancient origins dating back to the 11th century, a time when the bishops of Pisa ruled over the territories of Lucca, and in fact the same kind of pie can be found in Lucca, differing slightly in the filling, which calls for the addition of beet greens and soaked bread. In the town where it is most famous, Pontasserchio, it is usually made for April 28, the Patron Saint's Day, which thus became the "giorno dei becchi" that is, in the broad sense, the festival of betrayed husbands.

🍷 Colline Lucchesi Vin Santo Occhio di Pernice

PISTOIA AT THE TABLE

The city of Pistoia is a special case, closed off on one side by the Apennines and subordinated for years to the provinces of Lucca and Florence. After having managed during the Fascist period to become an independent province, it went on to develop an economy of its own based on the paper-making industry, on home furnishings and on nurseries (the important *Biennale of Flowers and Plants* is held in the city of Pescia), as well as tourism which makes use of the ski facilities found in the Montagna Pistoiese and Abetone, the thermal baths in and around Montecatini and a variety of minor attractions such as the *Pinocchio Park* dedicated to the famous puppet from Collodi. In addition, for music-lovers there is the event called *Pistoia Blues*, with famous international musicians featured each year. The city's gastronomic tradition is influenced by that of Florence and is characterized by a territory consisting mainly of mountains, with a cuisine that is one of the humblest and simplest in Tuscany, based primarily on essential ingredients such as olive oil and the genuine products of the earth; beans, vegetables (the **asparago gigante** of Pescia) and products of the woods such as chestnuts and mushrooms, as well as on the raising of farmyard animals. The ingredients are skillfully utilized to create few but important dishes such as **sugo all'anatra muta**, ancient soups such as that of the **carcerato** (jailed man) made of the interior organs of animals or the **erbucciata** with herbs and beans; **zuppa di pane fritta** based on stale homemade bread, and the savory **cioncia** made of veal scraps; and lastly, various kinds of polenta and porridge such as those **con le leghe** containing corn flour and beans. Famous also is the charcuterie, such as **biroldo**, which is also typical of the nearby Garfagnana area, and **mallegato,** both addressed to hearty eaters, being made of pork meat and blood.

Another hearty Tuscan dish, the best version of which is found here, is the so-called **frittata con gli zoccoli**, a quick, tasty, "frittata" made of eggs and "zoccoli", that is, lightly sautéed diced bacon or leftover boiled beef. Pontormo, the great sixteenth-century painter, is said to have doted on it.

Noteworthy among the DOC wines are Bianco della Valdinievole and its Vin Santo. As regards sweets, the question becomes interesting for the variety of the offer of delicious recipes typical of this area alone. They start with the famous **brigidini**, invented by mistake in the 14th century, and go on to the very particular, truly inimitable **cialde di Montecatini** containing almonds, and then the **necci** from the mountains, the Carnival ciambella known as **berlingozzo**, and still more, the **confetti a riccio** and the delectable **panforte glacé** with chocolate, whose ancient recipe is a well-guarded secret. Another dish to be sampled is **panatino**, a delicious sweet bread enriched with figs and nuts, Vin Santo and raisins. The specialties made with cocoa are equally famous and delicious (tarts, bars, cream to be spread on cakes or cookies, coated fruit, pralines) as are those containing coffee found at *Slitti*, the prize-winning Pistoia chocolate-maker (Via Francesca Sud, no. 1268, Monsummano Terme, PT).

GLOSSARY

Starters, snacks, savory pies and luncheon dishes

Biroldo and mallegato – Pork charcuterie made with the skin, the less noble parts and the blood, enriched with spices, raisins and pine nuts, dark in color with a sweetish flavor; there also exists a saltier version with the addition of cheese. It should be accompanied by Tuscan bread and a wine of the type Montecarlo Rosso or Carmignano rosé; or it may be sliced and cooked with oil in red wine.

Neccio – A kind of poor-man's crêpe, cooked in the typical "testi", made of chestnut flour, water and salt, shaped in the form of rolls and filled with a mixture of ricotta and Nutella®, or of charcuterie; note-worthy are the ones rolled around sausage.

Pasta and soups

Briciolata – A simple, tasty soup, a traditional dish of the Pistoian shepherds, made of ricotta, chicken broth and stale bread.

Carcerato – A humble soup from ancient tradition made of giblets and scraps of meat, stale bread and pecorino, cooked very slowly. Its name, 'jailbird soup', derives from the fact that prisons were often located in the vicinity of slaughterhouses, from which they received the scraps used to make this dish, the famous everyday fare of prisoners.

Minestra di pane – One of the most ancient soups of humble origin, made depending on the ingredients available at the moment, such as cabbage, beet greens, beans, potatoes and of course homemade bread. In the Middle Ages it was the typical food given to pilgrims traveling to Rome who stopped along the way.

Sugo all'anatra muta –A holiday sauce made with duck of the breed called "muta" because of its hoarse croak, used to dress such first courses as polenta and fresh pasta, traditionally prepared on July 25 on the occasion of the festivities for St. James, the city's patron saint, with homemade macaroni.

Zuppa con le leghe – A tasty soup containing corn flour, winter cabbage and Zolfini beans, called "con le leghe" (with bonds) because the ingredients all link so well together.

Zuppa di funghi porcini – A delicious soup containing porcini mushrooms, which must be as fresh as possible.

Meat, fish, and side dishes

Capretto al forno – A savory main dish, usually accompanied by roast potatoes or polenta. Typical of the winter months in the Pistoia mountains.

Cioncia – A stew made of veal scraps with tomatoes, herbs, wine and a great deal of hot red pepper, typical of the area around Pescia. Originally a humble dish, it has now been reassessed and inserted in the menus of the most famous restaurants in the territory. It requires long preparation and an elaborate cooking process, with the final addition of slices of homemade bread. Its name derives from the "conciatori", the tanners and leather-workers who invented this dish made of scraps left over from their work. It should be accompanied by either a white wine such as that of the Valdinievole, or a good Rosso di Carmignano.

Zimino di lampredotto – A succulent, savory dish for connoisseurs made of "lampredotto" (the final section of the stomach in cattle) stewed with beet greens or spinach according to the cooking method known as "in zimino". Cuttlefish and squid are also found cooked in this way.

Cakes, pies, cookies and liqueurs

Berlingozzo – An ancient, fragrant ring-shaped cake, already known in the 15th century, whose dough is kneaded for a long time with simple ingredients such as eggs, sugar, butter and flour, flavored with orange and baked in the oven. It was typical of Carnival Thursday.

Brigidino – A thin, crisp wafer with the flavor and taste of anise typical of the town of Lamporecchio, made of flour, sugar, eggs and aniseed. The wafers, of characteristic shape, were made in the past on a special plaque that impressed on them the design of a flower, more recently with a special machine always found moving from one town festival to another. Their history dates from 1500 when a nun in the Order of St. Bridget made a mistake in dosing the ingredients while preparing communion wafers for the convent. Excellent also as a snack eaten while taking a stroll, especially with ice cream.

Cialda di Montecatini – A large, crisp cookie formed of two crunchy wafers with a filling of almonds and sugar pounded together, known the world over for its absence of fats and preserving agents. The wafers were invented in the 1920s by a family of Jewish pastry-makers forced to immigrate during World War II, who left the recipe to the buyer of their pastry shop *Bargilli*, which still today, thanks to the heirs, safeguards the recipe and bakes these sweets according to the time-honored procedure; including their packaging in the typical tin boxes. They should be accompanied by sweet Vin Santo such as Chianti Classico Occhio di Pernice or alone for breakfast or tea, or with ice cream (Viale Grocco, no. 2, Montecatini Terme, PT).

Confetti a riccio – Typical of Pistoia, these candies made of vanilla-flavored sugar have an irregular spherical shape with characteristic wrinkled curls. They can be filled with almonds, chocolate, hazelnuts, candied fruit or anise. Their history is lost in time; they were even mentioned by Dante and were made for St. Joseph's Day. At weddings, they were thrown to the guests as a sign of joy.

Frittelle di castagne or "migliaccini" – Tasty fritters made of chestnut flour and water, to be tasted either as a sweet sprinkled with sugar or with charcuterie, typical of the Pistoian mountain area.

Panforte glacé – A round cake containing nuts and candied fruit, bound together by a solidification procedure, left to rest and then covered with melted chocolate and left to cool. Typical of Christmastime, they can be found in one of the city's chocolate shops that follows the ancient recipe (*Corsini,* Piazza S. Francesco, n. 42).

Recipes

Starters, snacks, savory pies and luncheon dishes

Neccio (Chestnut flour crêpes)

Utensils: wire whisk, bowl, crêpe pan
Preparation time: 5 min. + 30 min. resting time for the batter
Cooking time: 3-5 min. each
Ingredients per 4-6 persons:
– 1 ¾ cups of chestnut flour
– water or milk as required
– a pinch of salt
– ricotta, sugar for the filling

Preparation:

① Sift the flour into a bowl, add a pinch of salt and a little water or milk, mix with the wire whisk to form a batter that is rather soft but thick and smooth.

② Let the batter rest for 30 min.

③ Oil the pan and heat it; drop the batter in it a little at a time, using a medium-sized ladle.

④ Distribute the ladlefuls of batter evenly over the surface and cook 2-3 min. per side. Continue in this way until all of the batter is used up.

⑤ Serve while still hot, filling the necci with sugared ricotta or if desired with charcuterie, and rolling them around the filling.

In the past this simple focaccia was cooked in testi or in the typical iron implements between two dampened chestnut leaves to heighten the flavor. They were used as bread for shepherds and farmers, who filled them with cheese. Since the traditional implements are no longer available today, these crêpes can be made in an oiled crêpe pan with very low edges, turning them at least once. The grated rind of a lemon or orange can also be added to the batter.

🍷 Colline Lucchesi Vin Santo Occhio di Pernice, Montecarlo Vin Santo Amabile, Montecucco Sangiovese

Pasta and soups

Briciolata (Chicken soup with ricotta)

Utensils: 2 deep pots
Preparation time: 10 min.
Cooking time: 1 ½ hr. for the stock
Ingredients for 4 persons:
– ½ cup of fresh ricotta
– 6 cups of chicken stock (soup cube acceptable)
– 4 slices of stale bread
– olive oil, salt, nutmeg and pepper
Ingredients for the chicken stock:
– 2 lb. of chicken
– 1 onion
– 1 carrot
– 1 stalk of celery

Preparation:
① Place the chicken in a deep pot with the carrot, celery, onion, and a pinch of nutmeg (optional); salt and simmer for about 1 ½ hr. over very low heat. When done, strain the stock into another pot.
② Keep the stock over low heat; add the ricotta, crumbling it directly into the pot, and salt to taste. Meanwhile, toast the slices of bread and place them in the soup dishes.
③ Serve the soup hot in the dishes, ladled over the bread; dribble with olive oil and dust with pepper.
🍷 Montecarlo Rosso

Farinata con le leghe (Corn flour soup)

Utensils: deep pot, wire whisk
Preparation time: 20 min. + 1 night for soaking the beans
Cooking time: 80 min.
Ingredients for 4 persons:
– 1 ⅔ cups of dried "Zolfini" beans
– 2 lb. of winter cabbage
– 2 cups of corn flour
– 1 onion
– 1 carrot
– 1 clove of garlic
– 1 bunch of parsley, salt, pepper and olive oil

Preparation:

① Soak the beans overnight in a bowl of water.

② Boil the beans next day in a large pot of water; pass some of them through the food mill, reserving their cooking water. Clean the winter cabbage well and chop it coarsely.

③ Sauté in the pot the onion, garlic and carrot. Add the mashed beans with 8 cups of water and the winter cabbage; simmer for about 1 hour.

④ When the cabbage is done, sprinkle the corn flour into the pot, stirring constantly with the wire whisk to keep lumps from forming and cook for about 20 min. more.

⑤ Lastly, add the whole beans and adjust the salt. The porridge is done when it is thick but still soft.

⑥ Serve hot in soup dishes, preferably made of terracotta, or in plates, dribbled with olive oil and dusted with pepper.

🍷 Montecarlo Rosso

Meat, fish, and side dishes

Lampredotto in zimino ("Lampredotto" in tomato sauce)

Utensils: pan, large pan
Preparation time: 70 min.
Cooking time:
Ingredients for 4 persons:
– 1 ½ lb. of "lampredotto"
– ¾ lb. of beet greens
– 2 cups of canned tomatoes
– 4 tablespoons of grated parmigiano or pecorino
– 10 tablespoons of olive oil
– 2 cloves of garlic, one bunch of parsley
– salt, pepper
– fresh hot red pepper to taste

Preparation:

① Boil the beet greens in salted water, squeeze them and chop them coarsely; sauté them for a few minutes in a pan with a chopped clove of garlic and a few tablespoons of olive oil.

② Cut the "lampredotto" into strips about ⅓ in. wide.

③ In a pan (preferably terracotta) sauté and stir 1 whole clove of garlic with parsley, hot red pepper and more olive oil, removing the garlic before it turns brown.

④ Add the "lampredotto", stirring and letting it absorb the flavors for about 10 min., then add the tomatoes, salt to taste and cook for 30 min. over moderate heat.

⑤ Lastly, add the beet greens and cook another 10 min.

⑥ Serve hot with parmigiano and a dusting of pepper.

🍷 Carmignano Rosso

Cakes, pies and cookies

Berlingozzo (Ring-shaped cake)

Utensils: bowl, wire whisk, cake pan with hole in the middle
Preparation time: 15 min.
Cooking time: 50 min. in a moderate oven (350°F)
Ingredients for 6 persons:
– 3 ½ cups of flour
– 3 eggs
– 1 cup of sugar
– ½ cup of butter
– 1 packet of baking powder
– a pinch of salt
– rind of one lemon
– ¼ cup of milk or Vin Santo as preferred
– 1 teaspoon of aniseed (optional)

Preparation:
① With the wire whisk, beat the whole eggs with the sugar in a bowl to form a foamy mixture. Add the lemon rind and slowly add the butter melted over hot water; stir gently.

② Add the flour sifted together with the baking powder, stirring to keep lumps from forming. Stir in the milk or Vin Santo to form a soft batter.

③ Butter and flour the cake pan, pour the batter into it and bake in a preheated oven.

This ancient cake was already in use at the time of Cosimo I de' Medici, but it was eaten at the beginning of a meal and not as a dessert or a snack as it is today. It is also told that, on the day of Carnival Thursday the greediest inhabitants of the town of Lamporecchio, where this dish seems to have originated, went around with a cake of smaller size tied around their necks, as a prank before beginning the Lenten fast.

There also exist ring-shaped cookies of harder consistency called by the similar name of Berlingacci *flavored with spices (cinnamon, cloves and anise) which are usually dipped in Vin Santo.*

🍷 Vin Santo Bianco della Valdinievole Amabile

Frittelle di castagne o migliaccini (Chestnut flour fritters)

Utensils: wire whisk, bowl, deep pan
Preparation time: 5 min. + 30 min. resting time for the batter
Cooking time: 3 min. each fritter
Ingredients for 4-6 persons:
– 2 ½ cups of chestnut flour
– ½ cup of raisins
– 2 tablespoons of sugar
– ¼ cup of chopped pine nuts and walnuts
– water or milk as required
– ¼ cup of sweet liqueur in which to soak the raisins
– a pinch of salt
– oil for frying

Preparation:
① Sift the flour into a bowl, add a pinch of salt and a little water or milk and whip with a wire whisk to form a rather soft batter free of lumps. Add the chopped nuts and the raisins, which have previously been soaked in warm water and liqueur; stir and mix well.
② Let the batter rest for 30 min.
③ Heat the oil in the frying pan and cook the fritters a few at a time, dropping tablespoons of batter into the pan. Continue until all of the batter is used up.
④ Drain the fritters as they are done on paper towels.
⑤ Serve while still hot, sprinkled with sugar.

If desired, a few tablespoons of sugar and the grated rind of an orange can be added to the batter.

These scrumptious fritters are prepared in many parts of the region for Epiphany. They can also be served with fresh sugared ricotta as a topping.

🍷 Pomino Rosso Vin Santo Amabile

PRATO AT THE TABLE

Prato, sitting on the plain that stretches between the mountain chains of Calvana and Mount Montalbano, was linked to the city of Florence from the 14th century until 1992, when it became an independent province, encapsulating in its territory such important areas as that of Poggio a Caiano and Carmignano, interesting from the historical viewpoint and above all that of wine-growing, for the production of famous labels that have led to the founding of the *Museo della Vite e del Vino* (Museum of Grapes and Wine) at Carmignano.

An important textile centre already in Etruscan times, it is still today one of Italy's major industrial nodes. At the same time, an interesting cultural movement is developing in Prato, with the founding of the *Museo del Tessuto* (Textile Museum) – which conserves testimony ranging from ancient fabrics from pre-Colombian times ethnic ones to the 20th century – and the *Centro per l'Arte Contemporanea Luigi Pecci* (Luigi Pecci Contemporary Art Center) which displays works by great contemporary artists.

The city's culinary tradition has however managed to remain independent of the Florentine one. Although it makes use of the same ingredients shared by Tuscan cooking as a whole, it has managed to renovated the typical recipes. Here too we find the legacy of the farmers' traditional cooking, humble but rich in inventive expedients.

Meat processing holds an important place, with the production of famous charcuterie such as the **mortadella** of Prato**,** of ancient tradition, with its spicy flavor, cooked with the addition of Alkermes liqueur; and the one called **capocchia**, and then **finocchiona**, as well as various kinds of prosciutto, all to be tasted with the **bozza**, Prato's renowned bread that is strictly salt-free, one of the best breads in the whole region, baked in various shapes and ideal also combined with delicious jams and marmalades, such as the one made of the finest type of chestnuts, called marrons; and pork, which is also the basic ingredient of the soup called **tegamaccio**.

The recipe par excellence is **sedano alla pratese,** a dish that is very simple but also very tasty, consisting of tender stalks of celery filled with a veal stuffing. Equally famous are the **tortelli di patate** that here, as in Mugello, are served with meat sauce; but also to be tasted are the **stracci di pasta al sugo di papero** a true delicacy for lovers of old-time cooking.

White meats such as rabbit cooked in the dish called **coniglio rifatto** are also excellent. Coming closer to the classic Tuscan dishes are porridges such as the one made with winter cabbage; soups, bread soups and so on, up to dishes typical of the plain of Bisenzio such as **ranocchi fritti**, fried frog's legs, a specialty to which is dedicated a colorful summer fair. Among the cities of Tuscany, Prato stands at the top as regards the production of sweets. Its pastry-makers, having won numerous awards and international prizes, are in demand all over the word. For the last few years an event called *Dolcemente Prato* has been held annually, dedicated to national pastry-making; it attracts thousands of gourmets. Furthermore, a route leading from the Bisenzio valley to the hills of Montalbano, called *La Strada dei Biscotti* (The Cookie Road) has been delineated for the purpose of discovering and sampling the many products of the territory.

Noteworthy among the many and widely varied sweets are the **brutti ma buoni**, crunchy cookies, lumpy in shape but with a heart filled with almonds; the **Mantovana** cake made of flour, sugar and almonds, the **zuccherini di Vernio**, little doughnuts flavored with anise, and the 'rocks' of Calvana, fluffy cookies of various flavors; the **biscotti col riccio**, with chestnut flour, and the soft cookies called **amaretti di Carmignano**, also containing almonds; and again from Carmignano, the **picce di fico secco**, tasty dried figs, without forgetting the delicious **pesche,** a kind of soft cupcake filled with cream or chocolate.

But we would need a vast amount of time to adequately comment on what has become the very symbol of the city, the delicious finale to any dinner or supper (from the most domestic to the most formal): the **biscotti di Prato with Vin Santo**. These cookies boast a long history. An ancient recipe for them is conserved among the documents in the State Archives, although their origin dates from centuries further back. In the old days they were made only on Sunday, after having baked the bread for the week, with simple ingredients such as eggs, flour and almonds.

GLOSSARY

Pasta and soups

Farinata con il cavolo nero – A cold-weather soup made with winter cabbage and cornmeal, typical of the mountainous area and of humble farm cooking; it is found in many versions throughout the region.

Insalata di trippa – A tasty dish consisting of tripe and fresh seasonal vegetables, it makes a good first course or starter, ideal for summer picnics thanks to the freshness of its ingredients.

Tegamaccio – An ancient, humble dish linked to pig-slaughtering time. In the old days it was made with scraps of pork meat and blood. To make this savory stew today the preparation has been refined, also due to changing taste, using pork stew meat with the addition of tomatoes, wine and hot red pepper, and sometimes potatoes.

Tortelli di patate – Ravioli of fresh pasta in the shape of squares, filled with a mixture of potatoes flavored with nutmeg.

Meat, fish, and side dishes

Braciole di maiale con cavolo nero – A traditional country dish linked to the killing of the pig. It consists of pork chops cooked simply in a pan with winter cabbage.

Sedano alla pratese – A delicacy consisting of stalks of celery stuffed with a mixture of veal, mortadella or chicken livers, eggs and spices, fried and then stewed in a sauce of meat and tomatoes.

Stracci di pasta al sugo di papero – An excellent combination of irregularly shaped pasta dressed with duck sauce.

Cakes, pies and cookies

Amaretti di Carmignano – A very soft, rather small cookie with an intense flavor of the almonds of which it is made, served on the occasion of important festivities.

Carmignanini – Crisp cookies formed of two discs of short pastry made of rice flour and filled with fruit and fig jam, typical of the town of Carmignano.

Biscotti col riccio – Crisp cookies of elongated shape. They are worked in a special procedure that leaves the surface dotted with little pointed cones resembling the outer hull of a chestnut, giving rise to the name. Among the ingredients are chestnut flour and wheat flour, as well as butter and eggs. Unfortunately, the production of these cookies is limited today, although they were once very popular in the mountainous areas.

Biscotti di Prato – Sometimes erroneously called **cantucci** or **cantuccini** (from which they differ in size and ingredients), they are unleavened cookies whose recipe is lost in the night of time. Due to their simplicity, they are easy to make at home, with wonderful results.

These cookies were made with scraps, the remainder, or "cantuccio" of the dough left over from cutting out cookies and as such, they were bought by or given to the very poor. Various types are available, all delicious, although the originals, such as those from around Carmignano, are the best kind for dipping in a glass of good Vin Santo. Among the best shops selling boxes of these cookies are the legendary *Mattonella-Biscottificio Mattei* (Via Ricasoli, no. 20/22, Prato) and the *Antico Forno Santi* (Via Migliana, no. 156/158 Loc. Migliana Cantagallo, Prato and Via Nazionale, no. 121r, Florence).

Brutti ma buoni – Also called "Mandorlati di S. Clemente", these are round, lumpy cookies containing almonds, whipped egg whites and lemon rind. They are hard on the outside, with a soft, fragrant almond filling inside.

Mantovana di Prato – Soft, fluffy cake made of sugar, almonds, eggs and flour.

Pesche pratesi – A sweet formed of two dome-shaped cookies, which are first scooped out, then lightly sprinkled with Alkermes and lastly filled with "crema pasticcera" or chocolate. The original recipe dates from the 19th century.

Picce di fico secco di Carmignano – Tasty tidbits made of dried figs of the species that has been grown around Carmignano since the remote past. They are picked in late August and left to dry on reed mats according to a particular procedure that leaves them soft inside. After having been dried they are paired two by two, with aniseed inside. They are ideal as dessert, accompanied by dried fruit and Vin Santo, but are also good eaten with soft cheeses and honey, charcuterie such as Colonnata lard or streaky bacon. Famous not only in Italy but also abroad, they are found at the annual *Antica Fiera di Carmignano* (Ancient Fair of Carmignano) held the first Tuesday in December, to be tasted at Christmas, when their drying time is over.

Sassi della Calvana – Although their name, which means 'rocks', may be confusing, these are very soft cookies made of hazelnuts with the addition of various ingredients including Vin Santo, pine nuts, raisins, candied lemon rind and chestnut flour.

Tigliate – This treat, to be eaten leisurely at the hearthside, usually on All Saints' Day, among friends and family members, consists of simple boiled chestnuts flavored with dry fennel.

Zuccherini di Vernio – Ancient cookies made on the occasion of important festivities such as weddings, flavored with anise, containing yeast, butter and flour and covered with melted sugar that crystallizes to form a white coating. They are usually eaten for breakfast, dipped in milk, but also as dessert with a glass of Vin Santo.

Recipes

Pasta and soups

Farinata con il cavolo nero (Corn flour and winter cabbage porridge)

Utensils: large, deep pan
Preparation time: 20 min.
Cooking time: 80 min.
Ingredients for 4-6 persons:
– 2 bunches of winter cabbage (about 2 lbs.)
– 2 medium-sized red onions
– 2 cups of corn flour
– 1 tablespoon of tomato paste
– 2 hot red peppers
– ½ cup of olive oil
– 4 cups of hot water
– 4-6 slices of toasted Tuscan bread

Preparation:
① Heat the olive oil over low heat in the pan with 1 hot red pepper and the finely chopped onions, stirring to keep it from burning.
② Clean the cabbage well and chop it coarsely; add it to the onions and the hot red pepper and cook for 5 min.
③ Add the tomato paste and cook for another 5 min., stirring well; add the hot water. Cover and cook over moderate heat for 45 min.
④ Sprinkle the flour gradually into the pot, cook for 20 min. stirring constantly to keep lumps from forming. Add hot water if necessary.
⑤ Serve in terracotta bowls with a slice of toasted bread.
🍷 Montecarlo Rosso, Montepulciano Rosso

Tegamaccio (Pork stew)

Utensils: large pan, preferably terracotta
Preparation time: 30 min.
Cooking time: 45-50 min.
Ingredients for 6 persons:
– 1 lb. of mixed pork meats, preferably scraps
– 2 oz. of Colonnata lard
– 2 heads of garlic
– abundant rosemary
– 1 glass of Chianti red wine
– 4 ¾ cups of puréed tomatoes
– salt, pepper and hot red pepper and olive oil

Preparation:
① In the pan, sauté in abundant olive oil the meat with the garlic, rosemary, a little salt and pepper; brown for about 10 min.
② Add the red wine and let it evaporate, then add the puréed tomatoes and hot red pepper and cook covered for another 20-25 min. over moderate heat.
③ Serve the dish hot, garnished with slices of grilled polenta if desired.

The original recipe called for the blood of a freshly slaughtered pig in place of the red wine. To make this dish unique, cubed potatoes can be added along with the tomatoes.

🍷 Bolgheri Rosso, Barco Reale di Carmignano

Meat, fish, fried and side dishes

Braciole di maiale con il cavolo nero (Pork chops with winter cabbage)

Utensils: pan, deep pot
Preparation time: 10 min.
Cooking time: 20 min. for the cabbage + 20 min. for the meat
Ingredients per 4 persons:
– 4 pork chops
– 1 bunch of winter cabbage (about 1 lb.)
– 2 cloves of garlic
– 1 sprig of rosemary

– a little fresh fennel, salt, pepper and olive oil

Preparation:

① In a pan, heat the olive oil with the rosemary, garlic and fennel. After a few minutes, add the pork chops, salted and peppered, and cook for 15 min.

② Rinse the winter cabbage and boil it in abundant salted water.

③ Add the well-squeezed cabbage to the meat and cook over high heat for about 5 min., stirring to mingle the flavors.

④ Serve while still hot in individual dishes with a good sprinkling of pepper.

The typical and official version of the winter "smigliacciate", when at pig-killing time the farmers gathered in the homes to celebrate the occasion with hearty dishes flavored with good wine.

🍷 Pomino Rosso, S. Gimignano Rosso Novello, Carmignano Rosato

Polpette alla pratese (Meatballs Prato style)

Utensils: pan, deep pot

Preparation time: 30 min.

Cooking time: 5 min. for the scaloppine + 30 min. for the meat sauce + 20 min. for the meatballs

Ingredients for 4 persons:

– ½ lb. veal scaloppine
– ¼ lb. of bacon
– 2 large potatoes
– ½ cup of nutmeats
– 4 eggs
– ¼ cup of butter
– flour
– nutmeg, a bunch of parsley
– 2 cups of meat sauce
– 1 clove of garlic
– salt, pepper and olive oil

Ingredients for the meat sauce:

– 1 lb. of ground veal
– 2 cups of puréed tomatoes
– 1 onion, 1 carrot
– olive oil

Preparation:
① Boil the potatoes for 15-20 min. in a pot containing abundant salted water (or in a pressure cooker for 7 min. after the whistle starts), peel them and mash them.
② Finely chop the walnuts.
③ Brown the meat in a pan with the butter and garlic for 5 min., then chop it finely with the bacon.
④ To prepare the sauce, first sauté together the chopped onion and carrot, then ad the ground meat, brown it for a few minutes before adding the tomatoes. Cook over low heat for 20 min.
⑤ In a bowl, mix well the meat, potatoes, 2 eggs, chopped parsley, nutmeg and nutmeats; salt and pepper and stir well to amalgamate all of the ingredients.
⑥ Make smallish meatballs, dip them in flour and then in beaten egg. Fry them in abundant hot oil for 5 min., then drain well on paper towels.
⑦ Add the meatballs to the sauce and continue to cook for another 15 min.
⑧ Serve hot.

If desired, you can add to this mixture 1 tablespoon of raisins softened in water. For even tastier meatballs, add 2 tablespoons of grated parmigiano to the mixture.

For a lighter dish, the meatballs can be prepared without frying and without sauce, baked in a moderate oven (350°F) for about 20 min. until they are golden brown.

🍷 Colli dell'Etruria Centrale Novello, Carmignano Rosato

Sedano alla pratese (Stuffed celery Prato style)

Utensils: pot, large pan, frying pan, butcher's twine
Preparation time: 20 min.
Cooking time: 10 min. frying + 20 min in the sauce
Ingredients for 4 persons:
– 8 stalks of tender celery
– ¾ lb. of ground veal
– ⅓ lb. of chicken livers
– 3 eggs
– ¼ cup of grated parmigiano
– 1 clove of garlic

– nutmeg
– parsley
– salt and pepper
– ½ cup of flour
– ¼ cup of butter

Ingredients for the meat sauce:
– 1 lb. of ground veal
– 2 cups of puréed tomatoes
– 1 onion
– 1 carrot
– olive oil

Preparation:

① Clean the celery well, removing the tough outer fibers, and cut it into pieces about 3-4 in. long. Parboil them in a pot of salted water. Then let them cool covered with a kitchen cloth with a weight on it to eliminate the excess water.

② In a pan, sauté the chicken livers and ½ lb. of ground beef with the butter and onion for a few minutes. Let cool and add 1 egg, the parmigiano, nutmeg, salt, pepper and parsley; stir and mix well.

③ To make the sauce, finely chop the onion and carrot together, add the rest of the ground meat, sauté the mixture for a few minutes, then add the tomatoes and cook over low heat for 20 min.

④ Fill one of the pieces of celery with the mixture, pressing it down well. Cover it with a second piece of celery pressed down so that it sticks together. Continue in this way for the remaining pieces of celery.

⑤ Tie the coupled pieces of celery together with the butcher's twine, roll them first in flour and then in the other 2 beaten eggs; fry in deep oil.

⑥ Add the meat sauce to a pan with a little olive oil and the garlic. As soon it comes to the boil, add the fried celery and simmer covered over low heat for 20 min.

⑦ Serve the celery while it is still hot.

Instead of the chicken livers you may use ⅓ lb. of ground mortadella to be added to the ground veal before cooking, while for the meat sauce it is customary to use duck meat.

🍷 S. Gimignano Rosso Novello, Carmignano Rosato

Cakes, pies and cookies

Biscotti di Prato (Prato cookies)

Utensils: pan, breadboard, saucepan
Preparation time: 30 min.
Cooking time: 25 min. in a moderate oven (350°F)
Ingredients for 6 persons:
– 4 cups of flour type 00
– 1 ¼ cups of sugar
– ¾ cup of butter
– 1 ½ cups of sweet almonds

– 4 whole eggs
– 1 packet of baking powder
– ½ packet of vanilla flavoring
– grated lemon rind
– 1 pinch of salt

Preparation:

① Sift the flour into a cone on the breadboard. Melt the butter over hot water.

② Break 3 eggs into the flour, along with the sugar, lemon rind, vanilla flavoring, pinch of salt, melted butter and lastly the baking powder.

③ Knead well to form a soft dough, then add the almonds and knead again for a few minutes.

④ Divide the dough into cylinders about 14 in. long and 4 in. wide; place them on the buttered and floured oven tray. Bush the surface with egg and bake them in a preheated oven.

⑤ When done, remove from the oven and slice lengthwise while still hot to form cookies about ⅓ in. thick. For even crunchier cookies, put them back in the oven for 5 min.

This is one of the many versions of this famous sweet, which is also found in different flavors such as chocolate, apricot, figs, walnuts and rum.
The traditional ones are the best to be dipped in Vin Santo and are also suitable for use as the base for puddings such as Tiramisù and Bavarese, as well as for ice cream.

🍷 Vin Santo di Carmignano Occhio di Pernice, Vin Santo del Chianti Montalbano Secco

Brutti ma buoni ('Ugly but good' cookies)

Utensils: terracotta bowl, wire whisk, pan
Preparation time: 30 min.
Cooking time: 35-40 min. in a moderate oven (320°F)
Ingredients for 6-8 persons:
– 6 egg whites
– 4 cups of peeled almonds (a few bitter ones)
– 4 ½ cups of powdered sugar
– vanilla flavoring
– powdered spices: cinnamon, coriander, cloves
– orange rind
– a few drops of sweet liqueur type "Grand Marnier"
– powdered sugar to garnish

Preparation:
① Toast the almonds in the oven for 5 min. and chop them coarsely.

② With the wire whisk, whip the egg whites stiff; fold in the sugar a little at a time and stir to form an even cream. Add the almonds, spices, lemon rind and liqueur. Stir well but gently, to keep the whipped egg whites from falling.

③ Pour the mixture into a bowl and let it thicken over a pot of boiling water, stirring, for about 5 min.

④ With the aid of a tablespoon, form irregular balls of dough about 1-2 in. in diameter.

⑤ Place them in a buttered and floured pan and bake in a pre-heated oven for 35-40 min.

⑥ As soon as they are done, sprinkle them with powdered sugar. They are even better the next day.

Also called "Mandorlati di S. Clemente", they were created in the early 20th century, and are usually sold together with "Biscotti di Prato".

To make even more special cookies, use 2 cups of almonds and 2 cups of toasted hazelnuts; 5-6 bitter almonds can also be added to give the cookies a more tangy taste. The original recipe called for a thin wafer at the bottom of each cookie.

🍷 Aleatico dell'Elba

Mantovana di Prato (Almond cake)

Utensils: terracotta bowl, wire whisk, 8-9 in. round cake pan with removable edge
Preparation time: 25 min.
Cooking time: 30-35 min. in a moderate oven (350°F)
Ingredients for 6-8 persons:
– 1 cup of sugar
– ¾ cup of softened butter
– 2 cups of flour type 00
– 2 whole eggs
– 4 egg yolks
– ¾ cup of finely chopped toasted almonds
– 1 packet of vanilla-flavored baking powder
– 1 packet of vanilla flavoring
– orange rind
– powdered sugar
– 1 tablespoon of pine nuts (optional)

Preparation:

① Melt the butter over boiling water and let it cool slightly.

② Whip the two egg whites stiff. Gently fold in the six yolks one at a time, add the sugar and stir to form a light, soft cream.

③ Add the orange rind, the melted butter, some of the almonds and the sifted flour; mix well. Add the baking powder last.

④ Butter the cake pan, dust the edges with powdered sugar and scatter some of the almonds over the bottom. Pour in the batter and cover the surface with the remaining almonds. For the topping, 1 tablespoon of pine nuts can also be added to the almonds.

⑤ Bake for 30-35 min. without opening the oven door for the first 20 min. at least.

⑥ The cake is done when it has risen well. Check for doneness by sticking a toothpick into the middle; if it comes out clean, the cake is done.

⑦ Let the cake cool and serve it sprinkled with powdered sugar. It will be just as good the next day too.

Among the various legends on the origin of this ancient sweet, it is said to have been brought in the 19th century, by two nuns from Mantua who were traveling through Prato. In gratitude for the hospitality they had received, they gave one of the city's pastry-makers this recipe, which had been famous already at the time of Isabella d'Este, when it was called 'Paradise Cake' for its soft, fluffy texture.

🍷 Vin Santo di Carmignano Secco

Pesche pratesi (Prato 'peaches')

Utensils: bowl, pan, oven paper
Preparation time: 1 hr. + 2 hr. rising time
Cooking time: 15-20 min. in a moderate oven (350°F)
Ingredients for about 30 peaches:
– 3 ⅔ cups of cake flour type 00
– ½ cup of sugar
– ½ cup of butter
– 4 eggs
– 1 packet of vanilla-flavored baking powder
– a pinch of salt
– 1 small glass of anise-flavored liqueur

– Alkermes for dampening
– grated rind of 1 lemon

Ingredients for the cream:
– 2 cups of fresh whole milk
– grated rind of 1 organically-grown lemon
– ¾ cup of sugar
– 2 egg yolks
– ½ cup of flour type 00
– ½ teaspoon of potato starch

Preparation of the cream:
① Pour ½ cup of milk into a bowl; add the sugar and the lemon rind.
② In a separate bowl, add to the rest of the milk the egg yolks, flour and potato starch and whip together well.
③ Pour this mixture through a strainer into the milk containing the sugar and lemon rind.
④ Pour all of these ingredients into a pot and cook over low heat, stirring constantly to keep the cream from sticking, for about 20 min.
⑤ When the cream has thickened, remove it from the heat and let it cool (it can also be placed in the refrigerator).

Preparation of the dough:
① Place in a large bowl the sugar, eggs beaten separately with a pinch of salt, the butter softened over boiling water and the lemon rind. Sift the flour into it and stir well to blend the ingredients.
② Lastly, add the baking powder and the liqueur and knead well to form an even dough.
③ Form balls of dough ⅓ in. in diameter. Place them well separated in the pan, buttered and lined with oven paper.
④ With your thumb, make a small depression at the centre of each cookie, to be filled with cream.
⑤ Bake in a preheated oven for 15-20 min.
⑥ Remove the cookies from the oven and let them cool.
⑦ Dip them briefly, two at a time, in the Alkermes diluted with sugary water, then spread a teaspoon of the cream on one cookie and cover it with a second like a sandwich.
⑧ Roll the cookies in sugar and place them in paper cupcake

molds. Decorate them with sugar leaves, if available. Proceed in the same way for the rest of the cookies.
⑨ Refrigerate for about 1 hr. and serve.

This is a sweet created at the time of the Unification of Italy, when an imaginative cook, to celebrate the event, served these 'peaches' at a dinner of fervently patriotic citizens of Prato, with a tri-colored banner flying above them as decoration.
Making these delicious cookies is a long process, but the results are more than excellent. We also recommend filling some of them with chocolate cream or jam.

🍷 Vin Santo Pomino Rosso Amabile

Zuccherini di Vernio (Vernio sugar cookies)

Utensils: terracotta bowl, oven tray, saucepan, wooden spoon, oven grill
Preparation time: 30 min.
Cooking time: 15-20 min. in a moderate oven (350°F)
Ingredients for 6-8 persons:
– 4 cups of flour 00
– ¼ cup of butter at room temperature
– 4 eggs
– 1 ½ cups of sugar
– 1 packet of baking powder
– 1 tablespoon of aniseed
– ¼ cup of anise-flavored liqueur

Preparation:
① Mix in a bowl ½ cup of sugar with the rest of the ingredients. Knead the dough to form a compact mass.
② Form ring-shaped cookies about 1 ½ in. in diameter. Bake them in a preheated oven on the oven tray lined with lightly greased oven paper for about 15-20 min.
③ Meanwhile, melt the rest of the sugar with a little water in a saucepan, over low heat.
④ As soon as the sugar has melted, dip the cookies into it a few at time, stirring them with a wooden spoon. Place them on a rack to dry and serve cold.

🍷 Vin Santo del Chianti Montalbano Amabile

SIENA AT THE TABLE

Strolling through Siena means touching with your hand the Middle Ages, when the city reached its peak of splendor. This is one of the most particular places in the whole region. Visited every year by thousands of tourists, who flock here twice a year especially (on July 2 and August 16), it is literally packed with people come to watch the Palio, the ancient horse race that has been run for centuries and that involves the citizens all year round, not only for its organization and preparation, but also in the joyous banquets held in the streets as part of the festivities accompanying the event. The menus on these occasions are reserved to gourmets with hearty appetites, since they consist of dishes using every part of the pig, the interior organs of lamb and chickens, and so on. An important university centre, declared by Unesco *patrimonio dell'umanità*, Siena was a crossroads of thoroughfares and trade, as well as a major stopping place on the Via Francigena on the journey to Rome, offering never-failing welcome and hospitality to travelers and pilgrims. Today as then, its taverns and restaurants offer those who stop a triumph of flavors linked to the dishes of old tradition.

Here 'you eat well and you drink well' in a fusion of tastes and lovely views that opens the heart and the belly. The territory of Siena is a succession of breathtaking views amidst cypress trees, olive groves, distant parish churches, castles and rows of grapevines marching over the hills. Here even a simple snack of bread, salami and cheese, either "marzolino" or pecorino – outstanding those of the Crete Senesi, and that of Pienza in particular – assumes another significance if we pause to savor it before the vast green countryside and the towns clinging to the gentle hills of the Crete and of Chianti, emblems of Tuscany itself the world over: Buonconvento, Montepulciano, S. Quirico d'Orcia, Asciano, Monteriggioni, Pienza, Castelnuovo Berardenga, S. Gimignano and Castellina in Chianti, are only some of the marvelous localities to be seen, without forgetting the natural thermal baths of Chianciano, Rapolano, Bagno Vignoni and S. Casciano dei Bagni. Within the city of Siena are places deemed real temples to the ancient culinary tradition, where delicacies from all ages can still be found.

Sienese cuisine retains echoes of Medieval and Renaissance splendor, when banquets were based on meat and game highly flavored with the spices – the most commonly used, still today, being cinnamon, ginger, saffron, cloves and estragon – that arrived from distant lands, thanks to the city's merchants; while the more humble people found satisfaction in wild herbs picked in the fields and stale bread used for soups. Siena underwent long domination by Florence, which left an imprint on its cooking as well. It should also be remembered, however, that the most famous cooks at the Medici court came from Siena and it was very probably they who created dishes that were to become world-famous such as duck with sweet orange sauce, which then evolved into the better-known **anatra all'arancia** and the sweet called **zuppa del Duca** made of little cakes soaked in liqueur and covered with cream. But although Sienese cooking does not differ highly from that of Florence and despite the fact that it must satisfy the requisites of tourists, it manages to find a good compromise with innovation, while keeping its tradition vitally alive. Still today there remains the customary roasted and grilled meat, as well as stewed game, dressed with special sauces such as **lepre in dolceforte**, but also meat that is boiled as in **stiracchio** or stewed as in **scottiglia**. And here too it is easy to find steaks from cattle of the Chianina breed.

Another dish coming from the recipes of the people is **ginestrata**, a spiced soup that is a real pick-me-up made with eggs, stock and Vin Santo; and then there is **cipollata**.

Only in the last few years has one of the most ancient breeds of pig, already known in the Middle Ages, been rediscovered. This is the breed called **cinta senese**, very special pigs whose name derives from the distinctive light-colored band (the *cinta*, or belt) that runs around the animal's body. Living in a semi-wild state, these pigs feed on acorns, cereals, truffles and roots, which give their flesh flavor and fragrance. Excellent in fact are the prosciutto, salami, finocchiona and capocollo, as well as the **buristo**, from the cinta senese. This kind of charcuterie – some of which is found in other parts of Tuscany too – where it is also called **mallegato** and is enriched with other ingredients, as for instance in Pistoia with pine nuts and raisins – originated here in the 18th century, derived from the German würstel, to which the Sienese added spices. Recently reintroduced is the cultivation of **zafferano** (saffron) at S. Gimignano, grown there in the Middle Ages and so precious that it was also used to dye fabrics, in artists' paints, and in medicine, and even as a coin of exchange in trading. In the kitchen it is used in preparing sauces and creams for first courses such as **pici**, the pasta in the shape of long spaghetti found also at Grosseto, and even to flavor bread and the flat loaves called "schiacciata". In late October, the "Giallo come l'Oro" (Yellow as Gold) fair is held in the town, with the sampling of typical dishes.

Many are the sweets made for various occasions, such as **schiacciata di Pasqua** and **pan co' Santi** for All Saints' Day, although the best known are the Christmas ones such as **panforte**, **panpepato**, **ricciarelli**, and **cavallucci** exported all over the world, without forgetting such everyday treats as the ancient **torta dei medici** – meaning doctors, and not the famous Florentine family – which was prescribed as an invigorating tonic, made of spinach, honey, apples, almonds and spices; or **copate**, crisp delights containing honey and dried fruit. This part of the region also produces excellent wines, starting from the famous **Brunello di Montalcino**, ranging through **Chianti dei Colli Senesi**, **Vernaccia di S. Gimignano** and ending with the more recent **S. Antimo**.

GLOSSARY

Starters, snacks, savory pies and luncheon dishes

Ciancinfrincola – A tasty specialty whose curious name in dialect indicates something mingled in confusion. It is, in fact, a kind of sauce made of scrambled eggs sautéed with olive oil, garlic, black pepper or hot red pepper and a few tomatoes. It is ideal for spreading on slices of toasted bread.

Crostini bianchi – Rounds of bread with butter, cheese and trifola, or better still, white truffles. It originated in San Gimignano.

Crostini di milza e fegato – A classic Tuscan starter made of chicken liver and veal spleen cooked in wine, blended and spread on rounds of bread. The version in which the bread is first dampened with dry Vin Santo is used.

Fettunta con pecorino di Pienza – The traditional slice of toasted Tuscan bread rubbed with garlic, dressed with olive oil and accompanied by slices of one of the world's oldest and most famous pecorino cheeses. A very simple but remarkably satisfying snack.

Pasta and soups

Brodo con le cicche – A farmers' soup made with chicken stock in which the interior organs and chicken livers are cooked.

Cipollata – An onion soup flavored with lard and a hambone, known around Florence as **carabaccia**.

Ginestrata – A soup made of eggs, chicken stock, spices and Vin Santo. It has a curious history, being traditionally offered by a mother-in-law to her daughter-in-law when she entered her new home to spend her wedding night.

Pappardelle con la lepre – A classic of Tuscany cooking, but which here as in the Arezzo area finds its ideal scenario, made of very fresh game and just-made pasta in the form of "pappardelle".

Pici – In contending the origin of this particular type of pasta (*see photo p. 200*) with the nearby Grosseto, the Sienese have prepared unusual dressings, such as that of zucchini and saffron, in addition to classic sauces such as those made of meat, sausage or "all'aglione" with abundant garlic and tomatoes.

Stiracchio – A tasty dish made with leftover boiled meat, which is floured and sautéed, then plunged in a sauce of tomatoes and wine. It is served with pepper and a lot of bread.

Strisce e ceci – A richer version of the classic pasta and chick peas, here reinterpreted with partially puréed chick peas dressed with a savory sauce of tomatoes, onions and garlic in which are cooked the "strisce", pasta of the tagliatelle type but wider and more irregular in shape.

Zuppa senese di fagioli – Slices of stale bread are toasted, dressed with a few drops of olive oil and dusted with grated pecorino. A broth of Cannellini beans, flavored with olive oil, garlic and pepper, is poured over them.

Meat, fish, and side dishes

Arrosto morto – A dish influenced by Florentine cuisine, made of meat cooked simply with olive oil, garlic and some aromatic herbs.

Fegatelli di maiale alla senese – A very savory dish made of pork liver covered in pork membranes, flavored with lard, fennel seeds and lemon rind, and cooked in the oven. The dish is common to other parts of the region as well, with the variation of being cooked on skewers with bay leaves and orange rind, or as is customary in Prato, stewed in a pan with aromatic hers. It is frequently found as an ingredient of **spiedino alla senese** along with other meats, such as sausage and loin of pork, or as "uccellini" alternating with slices of toasted bread and bay leaves.

Lepre in dolceforte – One of the dishes inherited from the splendors of the Renaissance, consisting of hare that has been hung for a long time, dressed with a particular sweet-and-salty sauce containing onions, prosciutto, carrots, unsweetened chocolate, pine nuts, candied fruit and sugar. A curious and unusual combination, but a real must to be sampled in a local restaurant.

Scottiglia or **Buglione** – A stew made with various kinds of meat (chicken, rabbit, veal, pork, etc.) which are first sautéed and then cooked in a sauce of tomatoes, hot red pepper and red wine. This is a dish typical of the shepherds who brought their flocks from Casentino to the Maremma to graze. Different versions of this dish exist today, because it was made with the meat available at the moment.

Cakes, pies, cookies and liqueurs

Cavallucci – Cookies almost round in shape, ranging from soft to hard in consistency, made with walnuts, candied fruits, flour, honey, spices and wine, served with a glass of Vin Santo or Passito in which to dip them. Of very ancient origin, their name derives from the stable boys who took care of the horses at post stations, who consumed them in large quantities, also because they keep for a weeks at a time.

Ciambellino – One of the many existing versions of these cookies of humble Tuscan tradition is the one in which they are made of fried bread dough and coated with sugar, typical of Carnival time in Siena.

Copate – A sweet of ancient Arab origin, from which derives its name, formed of two wafers with a crunchy filling of almonds or walnuts and honey, flavored with anise. They are found in two versions: white (with almonds, honey and egg whites) and black (with finely chopped dried fruit, honey and cocoa).

Goglioli – A tastier version of the chestnuts "bruciate" over burning coals, in which they are sprinkled with Chianti red wine when almost done and are covered with a clean cloth before being eaten. Some cooks like to peel them and plunge them in a glass of red wine.

Pan co' Santi – This is a soft, sweet loaf from the humble foods tradition, prepared especially for the time around All Saints' Day, containing walnuts, raisins, flour and sugar and usually accompanied by the new wine taken from the wine barrels in early November.

Panforte – The classic version is a round, hard cake made of flour, almonds, spices, candied fruit and honey, resting on a base of thin wafers and sprinkled with cocoa. In the past it was made with sweet fruit – grapes, figs and apples – baked in the oven, to which flour was then added to form a dough. It did not last for a long time, and after a few days could take on an acid taste, and was called in fact "forte" (strong). There exists a more recent version containing chocolate.

Panforte Margherita or **Bianco** – This is a sweeter, more delicate version of the cake described above, from which it differs in containing more spices, candied citron instead of melon, and in being enriched with vanilla extract and powdered sugar sprinkled on top. It was created in 1879 in honor of Queen Margherita di Savoia, who came to Siena to see the Palio.

Panpepato – This sweet cake has the same basic ingredients as panforte, but with the addition of ground black pepper and at times of cocoa as well, making it truly special.

Its origin is lost in time, but it is known to have been baked for Christmas already in the 16th century. But its history is also linked to one of the many sieges undergone by the city. It is told in fact that a nun invented it, based on a "focaccia" with fruit similar to "panforte", a new sweet designed to stimulate the energy of the citizens by the addition of ginger, candied fruit and pepper.

Pinolata – A very simple Easter sweet made of flour, sugar, butter, eggs and pine nuts, flavored with lemon or orange, made either with or without cream.

Ricciarelli – One of the world's most famous Christmas cookies, made of marzipan, eggs, and honey flavored with vanilla. They have a characteristic diamond shape, with a cracked surface dusted with powdered sugar and are very soft. There also exists a version lightly coated in chocolate. Their origin dates from the time of the Crusades, when they were introduced into Siena by a crusader called Ricciardetto, for whom they were then named, who had first tasted them in the Holy Land.

Schiacciata di Pasqua – A soft, fluffy twice-risen cake traditionally served at Easter, made of flour, sugar and eggs flavored with mint liqueur, Vin Santo and orange juice. Its name derives from the custom of crushing eggs at the end of Lent.

Tegole di Montalcino – Cookies containing the famous wine with the addition of spices, eggs, sugar, flour and almonds, made according to a very ancient recipe.

Torta alla senese – Cake made with rice, milk, eggs, raisins and dried fruit, flavored with lemon.

Torta de' Medici – Formed of two disks of pie dough filled with a mixture of spinach, Tuscan mustard, sugar, candied oranges, eggs, raisins, macaroons, flour, dried fruit and spices. In the past it was filled with a mixture of honey, cooked apples, spinach, and almonds and covered with a crust made of bread dough.

Zuppa del Duca – Created in the 16th-17th century in honor of the Duke of Correggio or perhaps of Grand Duke Cosimo III de' Medici, this sweet – made of cream and ladyfingers dipped in Alkermes – is the first version of the more famous one that, brought to Florence, was renamed "zuppa inglese" (English pudding) because it was so popular among the British residing there.

Recipes

Starters, snacks, savory pies and luncheon dishes

Ciancinfricola (Eggs in tomato sauce)

Utensils: bowl, wire whisk, pan
Preparation time: 10 min.
Cooking time: 10 min.
Ingredients for 4 persons:
– 4 fresh eggs
– 1 clove of garlic
– 2 tablespoons of tomato paste
– 6 tablespoons of olive oil
– salt, black pepper or hot red pepper
– 4 slices of Tuscan bread

Preparation:
① Sauté the peeled and crushed garlic in the olive oil for a few minutes; remove it and add the tomato paste; cook for 2 min.
② Meanwhile, vigorously beat the eggs with a pinch of salt in the bowl.
③ Pour the eggs into the pan, stirring as for scrambled eggs.
④ Salt and pepper; cook until the eggs have solidified.
⑤ Serve on slices of toasted bread.

🍷 Vernaccia di S. Gimignano

Pasta and soups

Strisce e ceci (Pasta and chick peas)

Utensils: food mill, deep pot
Preparation time: 20 min.
Cooking time: 20 min.
Ingredients for 6 persons:
– 2 cups of precooked chickpeas with their cooking water
– ⅔ lb. of pasta type strisce (or non-egg pasta tagliatelle or "maltagliati")
– 4 medium-sized ripe tomatoes or 3 tablespoons of tomato paste dissolved in hot water
– 3 cloves of garlic

– ½ cup of olive oil
– 1 bunch of parsley, 1 sprig of rosemary
– salt and pepper

Preparation:

① Put half of the chickpeas with their cooking water through the food mill.

② Sauté the chopped garlic, rosemary and parsley in a pan for 2-3 min.

③ Add the puréed chickpeas and the whole ones and stir for a few minutes to let them absorb the flavors; then add the diced tomatoes, two or three ladlefuls of hot water and cook for about 15 min.

④ Add the pasta and cook for the time required for the type used. Salt and pepper.

⑤ Serve the soup when it has thickened slightly.

🍷 Rosso di Montepulciano, S. Gimignano Rosato

Meat, fish, and side dishes

Arrosto morto (Roast veal or pork)

Utensils: oven pan
Preparation time: 20 min.
Cooking time: 130 min.
Ingredients for 4 persons:
– 1 ¾ lb. of veal or pork
– 2 cups of vegetable stock made from soup cube
– 2 tablespoons of butter
– 1 oz. of diced bacon
– 1 onion, 1 carrot
– 1 stalk of celery
– 3 sprigs of rosemary and 3 of sage
– olive oil, salt and pepper

Preparation:

① Bind the meat with butcher's twine, inserting the sprigs of rosemary and the sage leaves.

② Brown the meat well in the pan with the butter and diced bacon; salt and pepper it.

③ Add the chopped herbs and sauté for a few minutes.

④ Add the vegetable stock and simmer over moderate heat for about 2 hr.

⑤ Serve the roast sliced, removing the twine and the herbs, accompanied by the vegetables.

The Tuscan term "arrosto morto" (literally, dead roast) *indicates that particular type of cooking meat not by roasting it on a spit but by simmering it in a mixture of chopped garlic and a few other herbs sautéed in olive oil. It was considered a Sunday dish, since a piece of meat was not always available everyday, and the ingredients were those of the household garden.*

🍷 Brunello di Montalcino, Sant'Antimo Novello

Stiracchio (Boiled beef in tomato sauce)

Utensils: casserole
Preparation time: 10 min.
Cooking time: 50 min.
Ingredients for 6 persons:
– 1 lb. of boiled meat (beef, veal)
– 2 white onions
– 2 cups of canned tomatoes
– 2 cloves of garlic
– a few leaves of sage
– olive oil
– salt and pepper
– grated parmigiano

Preparation:

① In the casserole, sauté the garlic and sage, add the sliced onions, cook until golden brown and then add the tomatoes. Salt, pepper, cover and cook for 30 min. over high heat.

② Cut the boiled meat into small pieces, add them to the sauce and cook for 15 min. until the meat begins to come to pieces.

③ Serve with a dusting of pepper and one of parmigiano.

🍷 Morellino di Scansano, Montepulciano Rosso

Cakes, pies and cookies

Cavallucci (Almond cookies)

Utensils: saucepan, breadboard, pan

Preparation time: 30 min.
Cooking time: 20 min. in a very low oven (250°F)
Ingredients for 20 cookies:
– 4 cups of flour type 00
– ¾ cup of sugar
– ¾ cup of blanched almonds
– ⅓ cup of acacia honey
– ¾ cup of candied fruit
– 1 ½ tablespoons of aniseed
– a sprinkling of cinnamon, nutmeg, cloves, coriander
– ½ a teaspoon of baking soda
– powdered sugar to garnish

Preparation:
① In a saucepan over low heat, warm the sugar with the honey and a tablespoon of water, stirring carefully with a wooden spoon.
② When bubbles begin to form on the surface, dip out a bit of the syrup on a toothpick and drop it in a cup of cold water; when it forms a soft ball, the syrup is done; remove it from the heat.
③ Cut the candied fruit into small pieces, blanch the almonds, toast them and chop them fine
④ Add the ingredients to the honey and sugar, mixing well.
⑤ Pour the mixture onto a floured breadboard, leveling it to a thickness of ½ to 1 in. and let it cool for 5 min.
⑥ Cut the dough and shape it into balls about 2-3 in. in diameter; flatten them slightly, place them in an oven pan lined with oven paper and bake for 20 min.
⑦ Serve cold sprinkled with powdered sugar.

A copper pan is best for melting the honey and sugar, but a sufficiently large non-stick pan can also be used.

🍷 Sparkling Bianco di Pitigliano, Vin Santo del Chianti Occhio di Pernice dei Colli Senese Sweet

Panforte casereccio (Spice cake)

Utensils: casserole, bowl, 9 in. cake pan with removable rim
Preparation time: 45 min.
Cooking time: 15 + 40 min.

Ingredients for 8 persons:
– 1 ¼ cups of flour type 00
– ½ cup of honey
– 1 ⅓ cups of powdered sugar
– 1 ⅓ cups of blanched almonds
– 1 cup of candied citron
– 1 cup of candied orange
– ¼ cup of powdered sugar
– vanilla flavoring

– 1 tablespoon of unsweetened cocoa
– powdered spices (coriander, cinnamon, cloves, nutmeg, ginger)
– powdered sugar to garnish, thin wafers

Preparation:
① Blanch the almonds in water, peel them and dry them in a hot oven (400°F) for a few minutes. Chop them fine and place them in the terracotta bowl.
② Coarsely chop the candied fruit and add it to the almonds; add the spices, the sifted flour and the other ingredients. Mix well and set aside.
③ In a saucepan over low heat, warm the sugar with the honey

and a tablespoon of water stirring carefully with a wooden spoon. When bubbles begin to form on the surface, dip out a bit of the syrup on a toothpick and drop it in a cup of cold water; when it forms a soft ball, the syrup is done; remove it from the heat.

④ Add the syrup to the almonds and candied fruit mixture; stir and mix well with a wooden spoon.

⑤ Butter the cake pan and line it with the wafers; pour in the mixture and level the surface with a wet knife. Sprinkle with powdered sugar and bake for 30 min.

⑥ Serve cold.

In one of the many versions of this spice cake, 1 cup of walnuts and 1 cup of hazelnuts are added to the almonds.

🍷 Vin Santo Amabile di S. Antimo

Pinolata (Pine nut cake)

Utensils: wire whisk, bowl, 10 in. round cake pan
Preparation time: 20 min.
Cooking time: 35 min. in a moderate oven
Ingredients for 6/8 persons:
– 2 ½ cups of flour type 00
– 4 eggs
– ⅔ cup of butter
– 1 ½ cups of pine nuts
– 1 ½ cups of sugar
– 1 lemon rind, 1 packet of baking powder
– vanilla flavoring
– 1 pinch of salt, powdered sugar to garnish

Preparation:
① Beat the egg yolks with the sugar, slowly add the butter melted over boiling water and the grated lemon rind. Stir well, then add the sifted flour. Mix well to form a firm but soft dough.

② Whip the egg whites with a pinch of salt until stiff; fold them delicately into the dough, stirring in one direction only to keep them from falling.

③ Lastly, stir in ¾ cup of pine nuts, the baking powder and vanilla flavoring, stir rapidly but gently and pour the dough into a buttered and floured cake pan.

④ Sprinkle the top with the remaining pine nuts and 3 tablespoons of sugar before placing in the oven to bake.
⑤ Serve the cake warm sprinkled with powdered sugar.

In the version with cream, half of the dough is poured into the cake pan and then covered with a "crema pasticcera", made of: ½ cup of milk at room temperature, a packet of vanilla flavoring, 1 tablespoon of flour, 1 egg yolk and ⅓ cup of pine nuts. All of the ingredients should be stirred well to form an even, rather firm cream.

The cream is poured over the first layer of cake dough, then covered with another layer, and more pine nuts are sprinkled on the surface.

🍷 Vin Santo, sparkling Moscadello di Montalcino

Ricciarelli di Siena (Traditional Siena cookies)

Utensils: blender, bowl, pan
Preparation time: 30 min.
Cooking time: 15-20 min. in a low oven (300°F)
Ingredients for 20 cookies:
– 3 ½ cups of hulled almonds
– 2 egg whites
– 1 cup of sugar
– ¼ cup of diced candied orange
– 1 grated orange rind
– 1 teaspoon of baking soda
– 1 ⅔ cups of powdered sugar
– 20 thin wafers (if unavailable, oven paper may be used instead)
– vanilla flavoring

Preparation:
① With the blender, blend the almonds with the sugar, the candied orange, the vanilla flavoring and the grated orange rind to form a rather coarse mixture.
② Whip the egg whites with a pinch of salt until stiff and fold them gently into the blended mixture.
③ Dip the mixture in powdered sugar. Shape the dough into the typical diamond shapes. Dip them in sugar again and flatten them lightly.
④ Arrange the cookies on the wafers placed on an oven tray covered with oven paper.

⑤ Dust them again with powdered sugar and bake for about 15-20 min.

To blanch the almonds, proceed as follows: plunge them into boiling water for a few seconds, then dry them in a hot oven for a few minutes. This is one of the many different versions of this famous sweet, one of which calls for no candied fruit but adds ¾ cup of pine nuts. Depending on individual preferences, all of the versions are worth trying. For true gourmands, the cookies can be covered with a chocolate icing, made by melting 3 ½ oz. of pure unsweetened chocolate over boiling water and dipping the biscuits into it one by one before baking as described above.

🍷 Moscadello di Montalcino, Vin Santo Amabile dei Colli Senese

Zuppa del Duca (The Duke's pudding)

Utensils: bowl, ceramic ovenproof pan
Preparation time: 15 min.
Cooking time: 15 min. for the cream
Ingredients for 6 persons:
– ½ lb. of ladyfingers or readymade sponge cake
– Alkermes for dipping as required
– whipped cream, sugared to taste
– slivered almonds to garnish

For the cream:
– ¾ cup of sugar
– 2 whole eggs
– 2 cups of milk
– 1 lemon rind

Preparation:
① To make the cream, put the ingredients in a saucepan and cook over low heat, stirring constantly to keep the mixture from sticking. When the cream becomes smooth and thick, remove it from the heat; remove the lemon rind and let the cream cool.
② Line the ovenproof pan with the ladyfingers. Sprinkle them with the Alkermes liqueur and pour the cream over them.
③ Cover with whipped cream and refrigerate for 2 hr.
④ Serve in fruit cups, garnished with almonds.

This is believed by some to be the primordial "tiramisù" exported from Florence to the Venetian court where, enriched with chocolate cream and dipped in coffee, it became fashionable for its aphrodisiac

effects. It was, in fact, rigorously consumed before an amorous encounter, giving origin to its name, literally "pull me up".

Sparkling Moscadello di Montalcino

Table of Contents

Index of recipes

Photographs:
11: Island of Capraia (LI); *48*: Arezzo. The Cathedral; *52*: Anghiari (AR); *62*: Florence. Ponte Vecchio; *90*: Braccio (GR); *96*: Pitigliano (GR); *103*: Massa Marittima (GR). The Cathedral; *104*: Livorno. Lungomare; *107*: Island of Elba (LI); *111*: Livorno. Medicean Port; *126*: Lucca. The Cathedral; *137*: Lucca. The Walls; *138*: Alpi Apuane; *144*: Alpi Apuane. Quarry; *156*: Pisa. The Cathedral; *172*: Pistoia. The Cathedral; *174*: Garfagnana (LU); *180*: Prato. The Cathedral; *182*: Poggio a Caiano (PO). Villa Medicea; *197*: Siena; *198*: S. Gimignano (SI); *211*: Pienza (SI); *212*: Impruneta (FI). Grape Festival.

printed in June 2008
by Genesi, Città di Castello
for
s i l l a b e